Emperor Haile Selassie

# OHIO SHORT HISTORIES OF AFRICA

This series of Ohio Short Histories of Africa is meant for those who are looking for a brief but lively introduction to a wide range of topics in African history, politics, and biography, written by some of the leading experts in their fields.

*Steve Biko*
by Lindy Wilson
ISBN: 978-0-8214-2025-6
e-ISBN: 978-0-8214-4441-2

*Spear of the Nation (Umkhonto weSizwe): South Africa's Liberation Army, 1960s–1990s*
by Janet Cherry
ISBN: 978-0-8214-2026-3
e-ISBN: 978-0-8214-4443-6

*Epidemics: The Story of South Africa's Five Most Lethal Human Diseases*
by Howard Phillips
ISBN: 978-0-8214-2028-7
e-ISBN: 978-0-8214-4442-9

*South Africa's Struggle for Human Rights*
by Saul Dubow
ISBN: 978-0-8214-2027-0
e-ISBN: 978-0-8214-4440-5

*San Rock Art*
by J.D. Lewis-Williams
ISBN: 978-0-8214-2045-4
e-ISBN: 978-0-8214-4458-0

*Ingrid Jonker: Poet under Apartheid*
by Louise Viljoen
ISBN: 978-0-8214-2048-5
e-ISBN: 978-0-8214-4460-3

*The ANC Youth League*
by Clive Glaser
ISBN: 978-0-8214-2044-7
e-ISBN: 978-0-8214-4457-3

*Govan Mbeki*
by Colin Bundy
ISBN: 978-0-8214-2046-1
e-ISBN: 978-0-8214-4459-7

*The Idea of the ANC*
by Anthony Butler
ISBN: 978-0-8214-2053-9
e-ISBN: 978-0-8214-4463-4

*Emperor Haile Selassie*
by Bereket Habte Selassie
ISBN: 978-0-8214-2127-7
e-ISBN: 978-0-8214-4508-2

*Thomas Sankara: An African Revolutionary*
by Ernest Harsch
ISBN: 978-0-8214-2126-0
e-ISBN: 978-0-8214-4507-5

*Patrice Lumumba*
by Georges Nzongola-Ntalaja
ISBN: 978-0-8214-2125-3
e-ISBN: 978-0-8214-4506-8

# Emperor Haile Selassie

Bereket Habte Selassie

OHIO UNIVERSITY PRESS

ATHENS

Ohio University Press, Athens, Ohio 45701
ohioswallow.com


Printed in the United States of America
Ohio University Press books are printed on acid-free paper ∞ ™

24 23 22 21 20 19 18 17 16 15 14 5 4 3 2 1

*Library of Congress Cataloging-in-Publication Data*
Bereket H. Selassie, author.
Emperor Haile Selassie / Bereket Habte Selassie.
pages cm. — (Ohio short histories of Africa)
ISBN 978-0-8214-2127-7 (pb : alk. paper) — ISBN 978-0-8214-4508-2 (pdf)
1. Haile Selassie I, Emperor of Ethiopia, 1892–1975. 2. Ethiopia—Kings and rulers—Biography. 3. Ethiopia—Politics and government—1889–1974. I. Title. II. Series: Ohio short histories of Africa.
DT387.7.B47 2014
963.055092—dc23

2014029648

Cover design by Joey Hi-Fi

# Contents

# Illustrations

# Preface

I must start by making a declaration that, beginning in the mid-1950s until the early 1970s, I served in the government of Emperor Haile Selassie. I served in different capacities, including holding the post of attorney general; thus I had ample opportunities to observe the emperor at work. Some portion of this book is, therefore, informed (and I hope enriched) by insights gained as a result of that experience. Nonetheless, for the most part I employed the usual research methodology of examining material about the emperor's life and work, principally biographical works, including the emperor's own two-volume autobiography.

It is tempting to write at length about the life and work of this historical figure of great fascination. Alas, the requisite size of this volume dictates concision; one has to be selective even in the works consulted, as the bibliography shows. The few pictures are chosen to represent different phases of the emperor's life. Then there is the English spelling of his name. Some use Haile Sellassie;

others Hayle Selase; others Hayla-Sellase. Here, as in all my writings about him, I follow the one used in the English translation of his autobiography—Haile Selassie. There are several different approaches to the spelling of Ethiopian names. The spellings I have adopted are, for the most part, sanctioned by use and should not occasion undue controversy. Titles like Ras and Dejasmach are written separately from the names; thus, Ras Imru should not be RasImru, and Dejasmach Balcha should not be DejasmachBalcha.

I must also note that I grew up hearing about Haile Selassie long before he changed his name, when he was still called by his given name, Tafari (he took the name Haile Selassie when he was crowned emperor in 1930). During my childhood in my Eritrean homeland, which was an Italian colony until 1941, my father and some of his close friends used to whisper his name and even quietly sing songs of praise, such as "Etiopia tenageri: bniguski bteferi" (Speak, O Ethiopia: speak in the name of your king, Tafari). As I mention in my memoirs, "Tafari was his given name . . . it was with the name Tafari that he had become well known as a popular and progressive ruler. His fame had spread across the Ethiopian border, to the then Italian colony of Eritrea and beyond, as the cult of Rastafarianism (Rastas) demonstrates."[1] Thus, I will say more on this and other aspects of his extraordinary life and work.

Of the biographical data that I consulted, none are more important than the memoir (in Amharic) of Ras

Imru Haile Selassie, *Kayehut, Kemastawsew.* Ras Imru was the emperor's cousin and close confidant, and was at his side, in good as well as bad times, from childhood through the stormy years of his feud with Lij Iassu until he assumed supreme power as emperor in 1930, and thereafter. Imru was with him during the last, fateful moment in September 1974 when a unit of the military junta, the Dergue, burst into the imperial palace and its leader informed the emperor that they had come to take him to a place of detention. The stunned emperor was speechless, whereupon Ras Imru intervened and was heard quietly counseling him to accept the inevitable gracefully. Then they led the once all-powerful monarch to an awaiting Volkswagen Beetle and drove him away as the jeering crowd shouted, "Leba! Leba! Leba!" (Robber! Robber! Robber!).

Thus ended a glorious reign, in ignominy. As historians have said about the passing of a Caesar, *Sic transit gloria mundi!*

Before deposing the emperor, the Dergue had asked Ras Imru to persuade his royal cousin, who had become their virtual prisoner, to provide them with information about his foreign bank accounts. The emperor was not willing to oblige the usurpers; through Ras Imru, he told them that if they could find any foreign bank account in his name, they were welcome to it! As this book will show, the Lion of Judah was nothing if not willful and tenacious, and he remained thus to the bitter end.[2]

Here a word is in order on the illustrious Ras Imru. I knew and greatly admired Ras Imru, not least because he interceded on my behalf at a time of my "troubles" with the emperor. He was universally loved and admired by the Ethiopian public for his uprightness and progressive politics as well as for his heroic role during the Italo-Ethiopian war of 1936. After Ethiopia's defeat, he was taken to Italy as a prisoner of war and spent five years in an Italian prison on the island of Panza.

His memoir is a priceless gem, containing as it does valuable information and insight on events and issues touching on the emperor's life and work. The editor of the memoirs says in the foreword that aspects of Ras Imru's descriptions in his memoir "have infused the raw material of history with a corporeal substance, making it breathe and smell human."[3] It is an apt and poignant remark. Ras Imru's memoir paints an intimate portrait of Haile Selassie as if he were his alter ego. It is an authentic testimonial of a life that was at once glorious and tragic.

The aim of this book is to give an account of the rise and fall of one of the twentieth century's truly remarkable leaders. Long before the rise in Africa of such men as Nkrumah and Nyerere—indeed, when most of them were still students—Haile Selassie had become world renowned. As the head of Africa's only (truly) independent nation, the emperor exerted considerable influence on Africans on the continent as well as those in the Diaspora. And when Italy invaded Ethiopia, Africans shared the sense of loss, as Nkrumah, Mandela, and others have written. When the emperor appeared at the League of Nations in Geneva to plead his people's case, he had become a world figure of no mean importance, as we shall see.

As part of the Ohio Short Histories of Africa series, this book is designed to provide a concise but well-rounded account of the emperor's life and work—his birth into the royal lineage, his struggle to attain the imperial throne, his championing of his country's modernization, and the challenges he faced through it all. His triumph and his tragedy.

1

# Leadership in the Context of Ethiopian History and Mythology

## The Question of Legitimacy

> By virtue of His Imperial Blood, as well as by the anointing He has received, the person of the Emperor is sacred, His dignity is inviolable and His power indisputable.

The words above are from Article 4 of the Revised Constitution of Ethiopia (1955). The same constitution also codifies the oral tradition according to which legitimate claim to the Ethiopian throne depended on the claimant's ability to trace his genealogy to the Solomonic dynasty, which was purportedly established by the union of King Solomon of Israel and the Queen of Sheba of Ethiopia through their son, King Menelik I, who was born during the queen's visit to behold Solomon's fabled wisdom.

For most Ethiopians, when they proudly spoke of their country's three-thousand-year history, that union loomed large, as, by some accounts, it did in the young mind of

Tafari Makonnen, the future Emperor Haile Selassie. This point is underscored by some of the emperor's biographers, who contend that belief in his dynastic genealogy gave him confidence that he was the legitimate heir to the throne of the ailing Emperor Menelik II, at a time when the question of who would succeed Menelik was an issue of momentous significance, as we shall see. Nonetheless, in his quest for the imperial throne, Tafari did not lie low, depending only on such claims of legitimacy; on the contrary, as we shall see, Tafari single-mindedly applied his indomitable will, political skills, and enormous energy to manipulate people and events toward the attainment of his goal.

As to the real basis of the story and whether the claim can be historically proved, that is immaterial. If the story is indeed based on myth, its durability shows the role of myth in history and society. The mythology of the Solomonic dynasty, believed by its originators to be based on history, acted as a powerful substitute for historical fact.

Belief was all.

This raises the question, why was it necessary for Ethiopian kings to rest their claim as legitimate heirs to the throne on such a story? Why would an African people insist on basing the legitimacy of their royalty on a story which happened long ago in a faraway land?[1]

Add to this the official title of the Ethiopian emperor—"the Conquering Lion of Judah"—and the puzzle becomes a mystery. In fact, that title provides the key to understanding why Ethiopians resorted to the Solomonic dynasty as a source of the legitimacy of their kings. Two biblical references are relevant here. The first is Matthew 1:1–17, which tells the story of the genealogy of Jesus Christ, "the son of David, the son of Abraham." The second is Revelations, which describes Jesus Christ as the conquering Lion of Judah: "And I saw in the right hand of Him who sat on the throne a book written inside and on the back, sealed up with seven seals" (5:1). "And I began to weep greatly," says John, the writer of Revelations, "because no one was found worthy to open the book, or to look into it. And one of the elders said to me, 'Stop weeping; behold the Lion that is from the tribe of Judah, the Root of David, has overcome so as to open the book and its seven seals" (5:4–5).

The relation between church and state has been a constant theme since the coming of Christianity to Ethiopia in the fourth century AD. Together, they conspired to elevate the notion of legitimacy based on the Solomonic dynasty as a defining principle of royal succession. According to some writers, the Ethiopians, or rather their ingenious scribes, penned the *Kebra Nagast*, the first written work to tell the story of the union between Solomon and Sheba, which also links the Ethiopian monarchy to Jesus Christ. Hence the critical relevance of the reference to Matthew's Gospel and Revelations. Some have further claimed that the Jews, by crucifying Jesus Christ, had relinquished their privileged position as God's chosen people and been replaced by the Ethiopians. Would this make such claimants “uppity wannabes,” to use a much-abused colloquial phrase? Is such a claim far-fetched? No more far-fetched than the idea of the Solomonic dynasty. But I digress, and I will not push the argument one way or the other.

We shall see the relevance of the Solomonic dynasty in the contest over who would be the rightful heir to the great Emperor Menelik II—would it be Tafari or others? But for now we will leave it there and proceed with the narrative of Haile Selassie’s life and work.

**A Man of Destiny**

Emperor Haile Selassie is one of the twentieth century’s illustrious leaders, who won almost universal accolades for bringing Ethiopia kicking and screaming (according to some) from tradition-bound backwardness to the light of modern times.[2] Several biographies have been written about him, in addition to his two-volume autobiography, and a growing number of memoirs, including some by former members of his government, have started appearing, attesting to the fascination he still inspires. Many of these memoirs are critical of his failings while lamenting the tragic manner of his demise, if not the end of his regime. One Ethiopian writer, a former functionary of his government, has faulted him for neglecting the nation’s interest in favor of his own selfish ends.[3]

In this volume, I attempt to focus on the core elements of his contributions as well as his failings. He was an enlightened monarch, but his earlier promise was unfulfilled and his historical legacy and stature have been diminished by his inordinate concentration and exercise of absolute power. Those who value the modernizing aspect of his work, however, may well argue that without that power he could not have accomplished his aim of modernizing Ethiopia. This is obviously a controversial issue, and I hope to address it below.

## The Context

As we assess Haile Selassie's role in modernizing Ethiopia, it is worth bearing in mind that he was a product of his country's history and culture. Needless to say, there is no value without context; and the core values that he imbibed from childhood, which affected much of his work, were rooted in the specific historical and cultural context of Ethiopia, with Christianity a dominant factor in that context. Some of those received values the emperor rejected and sought to change or abolish, such as the hated practice of slavery. He was also actively engaged in promoting modern ideas and institutions, which he would use as instruments in centralizing state power. As both the product of a traditional polity and the beneficiary of a modicum of modern education, he often found himself in the middle of heated controversies occasioned by a clash of values, which more often than not involved conflicting interests. Indeed, his modernizing blueprint, particularly as embodied in much of the 1931 constitution, was aimed at, and partially succeeded in, diminishing the powers of the potentates in favor of a centralized modern national state apparatus.

A prime example of such a clash was the feud between Menelik's grandson Lij Iassu (b. 1894) and Haile Selassie, then known by his given name, Tafari. The feud had degenerated into an open military confrontation in 1916, which ended in Lij Iassu's defeat and the triumph of Tafari and his "modernizing party." That triumph, which will be described in more detail in chapter 4, was a crucial blow for progress and enlightenment. It meant the introduction of more modern education and the start of the building of infrastructures befitting a modern state.

Both before and after ascending to the imperial throne, Tafari faced incredible challenges. How he met those challenges, sometimes with success, other times suffering temporary setbacks, is a story that reflects his remarkable political skills and his dogged determination to impose his will on a backward nation.

## The Ethiopian State

What is the core essence of the Ethiopian polity that Haile Selassie inherited? To answer this question, it is necessary to make reference to three related historical facts.

The first concerns the Christian origin of the state, which began in the fourth century AD with the conversion of the Axumite kingdom to Christianity.

The second is the expansion and consolidation of the Christian state, incorporating a wide variety of linguistic, cultural, and ethnic groups. The expansion continued for centuries until it reached its apogee by the end of the nineteenth century with Emperor Menelik's conquests, which expanded the state to include much of present-day Ethiopia, adding more territory and different ethnic groups and making the country an empire-state.

The third concerns the emergence of Islam in the seventh century AD. As it spread in and around the Horn of Africa subregion, including around Ethiopia, the challenge it posed to the Ethiopian state led to religious (Christian) nationalism becoming, in reaction, the defining characteristic of the Ethiopian state. The first serious threat to the survival of the Ethiopian Christian state was the Ahmed Gragne campaign in the sixteenth century. Although the state survived politically, Ethiopia's complexity in social and cultural terms originates in the Ahmed Gragne campaign and its aftermath. As the religion of a significant proportion of the Ethiopian people, Islam is an important part of the complexity—indeed, the richness—of the Ethiopian sociocultural reality. Moreover, the influx of the Oromo, who would become the single most numerous ethnic group in the country, into much of central and northern Ethiopia after the Gragne campaign added to the country's demographic and ethnolinguistic complexity.

A fact of great political significance in contemporary Ethiopia is that until recently the core of the state remained a monopoly of one ethnic group. At the center was the king, professing the Orthodox Christian faith and provided by the church with ideological backing in return for economic support, principally in the form of land grants and related privileges. The church-state coexistence, with the armed forces and bureaucratic apparatus providing, respectively, security and administrative structure, is the historic Ethiopian version of what is known in Egypt these days as the "deep state."

The crisis during the pre-1916 coup d'état, particularly as it concerned the Islamic sympathies and predilections of Lij Iassu, was a twentieth-century version of the Islamic challenge to the deep state, and the deep state's response resulted in Lij Iassu's overthrow, as we shall see in chapter 4.

# 2

# Tafari

## *Orphaned Prince Steeled by Adversity*

Tafari was born in the village of Ejersa Goro, five kilometers east of the city of Harar, to Leul (Prince) Ras Makonnen, a devoted cousin and trusted servant of Emperor Menelik, and Woizero Yeshimebet. Ras Makonnen took mother and child to his palace in Harar, where he was governor-general. Woizero Yeshimebet died delivering her second child a year and a half after Tafari was born.

When Tafari was four years old, Ras Makonnen decided to relocate him and his cousin Imru (later Ras), who was of the same age and also an orphan, to the small town of Kombolsha, not far from Harar. They lived in a gated compound under the watchful eyes of women guardians, who no doubt provided the missing maternal element to both children. Soldiers guarded their residence, and the boys were allowed to venture outside the compound only with the permission and in the company of their guardians. At age five, they were introduced to traditional Ethiopian studies, reading and writing Amharic and Geez, as well as studying the Psalms and *Melk'a*

*Mariam* and *Melk'a Yesus* (Life of Mary and Life of Jesus). Their Amharic and Geez teacher was Memh'r (teacher) Woldekidan, who on one memorable occasion took them to meet and receive the blessing of Abune Yohannes, a Coptic (Egyptian) bishop.

Ras Makonnen traveled frequently as Menelik's emissary to Europe. On the rare moments of his return, he would send for the boys to visit him in his government house in Harar, where they enjoyed his warm fatherly company for a few days. It is easy to imagine how much Tafari missed his father, to whom he was very much attached. At age eight, the boys were relocated to Harar to live in a more pleasant environment in a much larger house with more amenities. There they continued the traditional Ethiopian education that they had begun in Kombolsha, to which were added other subjects in a normal school curriculum, including learning French. Their teacher, who also acted as their guardian, was Dr. Vitalia, whom Ras Makonnen had brought from France for the purpose. Another teacher was an Ethiopian Catholic cleric named Aba (Father) Samuel, who belonged to the Catholic Mission of Aba Indrias. Between the two of them, the teachers organized morning and afternoon classes, alternating between French and other academic subjects, including reading and writing Amharic. In his memoirs, Ras Imru remembers with fondness the happy times they passed at the school, where they were also given riding lessons once a week. Ras Makonnen's decision to import teachers to instruct Tafari and other children of the nobility in Harar was a reflection of the larger program of modernization introduced by Menelik, which Makonnen earnestly emulated.

Some accounts of Tafari's childhood education contend that from the age of seven, when he first started to read and write Amharic, he seems to have become aware that he would one day succeed Menelik as a ruler of Ethiopia. He demanded from his Amharic tutor all the available books on Ethiopian history, and listened avidly to tales of the Solomonic dynasty, of which he understood himself to be an offshoot. By the time he was eleven, he had learned enough French to converse with Aba Samuel. His father proudly told Menelik about it, and Menelik, curious, requested that Tafari be brought to his court.

The introduction of modern education to Ethiopia under Menelik was accompanied by other modernization projects, including in particular the expansion of infrastructure. In this respect the Franco-Ethiopian Railway, running from Djibouti to Addis Ababa, was the most important, not only because it facilitated the expansion of trade and investment, but because it exposed Ethiopians to the rest of the world and opened it up to modern values and institutions, including banking and an early appreciation of the value of money. An illustration of this is the fact that Ras Makonnen opened a bank account abroad, as Tafari would do later when he became regent and crown prince.

## Conditioned by Adversity

Ras Makonnen died suddenly in 1905. The loss of the popular governor of Harar hit his admirers and supporters hard, and none was more affected than the young prince, deprived of his one surviving parent, who had acted as both mother and father to him. A touching photograph of Ras Makonnen and young Tafari, taken a couple of years before Makonnen's death, shows deep filial attachment. In his memoirs, Ras Imru gives dramatic descriptions of the public reaction to Makonnen's death, including the colorful ceremonies of his funeral and the wailing and demonstrations of loyalty exhibited by his servants and all the grandees of Harar.

In all the public display of support for and commiseration with the young Tafari, who had just turned thirteen, he maintained the stoic self-control and discipline that would mark his behavior throughout his life and illustrious career. His quiet and calm behavior throughout the public mourning, which lasted over a week, impressed all observers. It was as if he had been prepared for yet another misfortune and had steeled himself for it. Ras Makonnen's frequent travels must have added poignancy to the motherless prince's loneliness, but at the same time they must have helped prepare him for the tough years ahead, which would involve him in the deadly feuds between the contending forces in Menelik's palace and elsewhere in the empire.

3

# Harar, Ras Makonnen, and Menelik's Court

## Harar: Model Province of the Empire

In the last decades of Menelik's imperial expansion campaign, Harar was the crown jewel of the empire. In terms of the advent of modern ideas and institutions, it had become the leading city in Ethiopia. Following in the footsteps of his imperial predecessor, Emperor Yohannes, Menelik snatched Harar from the Harar city-state, ruled by Emir Abdullahi. After the decisive battle of Chelenko in 1887, when Menelik's victorious forces occupied the city and all the surrounding area of what is today Harar region,[1] Menelik appointed his cousin, Ras Makonnen, as Harar's governor. Tafari's birth in Harar was thus a consequence of that appointment.

The Harar region, with its diverse topography and great geographical contrasts, is a microcosm of Ethiopia. Lying on the eastern part of the country, Harar is bordered by Djibouti to the east and Somalia to the east and southeast. To its west it is bordered by the Shoa and Arsi regions, and to its south and southwest lies Bale. Its most distinctive features are a highland zone with temperate climate, as well as an arid zone stretching to the east.

Ras Makonnen was, by most accounts, a popular governor, who administered Harar with a firm hand but with justice and fairness, especially in regard to the way his minions, the empire's agents, treated the "conquered" peasantry. Makonnen also played a significant role in rallying thousands of the best regiments from Harar, forces that played a key role in Menelik's victory over the Italians at the historic battle of Adua in 1896. He was also a top advisor and close confidant of Menelik, who sent him as his envoy to special occasions such as coronations as well as to negotiate treaties on his behalf. In today's parlance, he would be minister of foreign affairs. In 1902, Makonnen made his second trip to Europe as Menelik's envoy to attend the coronation of King Edward VII of England. Such exposure to Europe reinforced his desire for modernization. As already noted, Menelik, on being told how well Tafari spoke French, had had the boy brought to Addis Ababa. At Menelik's court, Tafari conversed with a French-speaking diplomat. Menelik was duly impressed not only by the boy's fluency in French, which the diplomat confirmed, but by his confident conduct. Menelik, evidently seeing brightness and promise in the young boy, ordered that he attend the court to learn about royal governance, and also that he enroll in the newly opened Menelik School.

Makonnen was so close to Menelik that many considered him a possible successor to the imperial throne after Menelik's death. It is also likely that Makonnen himself entertained that idea. That may be why he appointed Tafari as Dejasmach (military commander) when he was thirteen years old, in the expectation, shared by Makonnen's party of modernizers and all Harar grandees, that Menelik would make Makonnen his successor and that Tafari would then be in a position to succeed his father.

Alas, that was not to be. Makonnen's sudden death proved a deadly blow to such expectations, opening the question of succession to more dramatic controversies, court intrigues, and infighting, which would eventually be resolved by military confrontation and war. Any idea that Tafari's brightness and Menelik's favorable regard toward him and his father might automatically entitle Tafari to succeed to Menelik's throne seemed to be relegated to oblivion. At least so it seemed at first.

### Menelik's Court before and after His Death

Just as there were people who wanted Makonnen to succeed Menelik, there were also those at Menelik's court who were pleased at Makonnen's death. Of the latter, the two most important were Menelik's wife, Empress Taitu, and King Michael of Wollo, father of Lij Iassu. Taitu had her own ambition of succeeding her ailing husband, and King Michael wanted his son, who was Menelik's grandson through his mother, to become emperor. Both Taitu and Michael knew that if Makonnen attained the throne, Tafari would eventually succeed him, dealing a deadly blow to their aspirations.

Then Menelik suffered his first stroke. Upon his recovery, he summoned Tafari from Harar and on November 1, 1905, appointed him governor of Selale, an important district in the central province of Shoa. Tafari, aged thirteen, administered Selale by proxy and remained at the court, where over the next few years he learned the art of government. He was also, by acutely observing instructive cases of court intrigue, studying and making mental note of schemers, connivers, and plotters, learning the art of survival.

To the surprise of many, Menelik decided to appoint Lij Iassu his successor under the guardianship of a trusted warlord, Ras Bitwoded Tesemma. The records do not indicate how Menelik's unexpected decision affected Tafari. But one can speculate as to how disappointed he must have been, particularly when Iassu's behavior and poor performance in governing became an open secret and were widely resented. Menelik then suffered a second stroke, after which his wife and some of her court allies ruled in his name for a short while. This development did not sit well with most of those in Menelik's court and the provincial potentates (Rases) with their own militia as well as other men of influence, whom we can call power brokers.

When Ras Bitwoded Tesemma died in 1911, Iassu, still a teenager, was free to assert his power. Encouraged by

Empress Taitu, he indulged in acts of debauchery and brutality, while completely neglecting his governing duties. Effective central government disappeared. Then, following a third stroke, Menelik died in 1913. Taitu engaged in power manipulation, dismissing people appointed by Menelik and replacing them with her own kinsmen from the north. Tafari was by then a very mature and generally well-regarded man of twenty-one, but Iassu's supporters and Iassu himself did not look on him with favor. Tafari had to walk a fine line between appearing loyal to Menelik's chosen successor and at the same time monitoring the situation like an eagle surveying a field filled with innocent sheep abandoned by their shepherd.

The ambitious Empress Taitu sealed her fate by overstepping her bounds, causing a decisive reaction against her by the ministers appointed by Menelik. The ministers, who represented the general sentiment of the Shoan ruling group, ousted Taitu and banished her to live a life of penance near a church around Entoto Mountain.

# 4

# The Feud with Iassu—the Plot Thickens

Before her ouster from power, one of Empress Taitu's significant acts was to appoint Dejasmach Tafari as governor of Harar, to the general applause of the modernizing forces in Ethiopia. The Shoan ministers who overthrew Taitu canceled all her appointments, save that of Tafari; in fact, they reviewed his case and publicly confirmed it sending him to his father's domain with added prestige and power to continue the modernizing programs that had been started by his father. Ras Imru, who was a key figure in Tafari's camp and part of Harar's governing establishment, recorded the details of some of the modernizing programs, including administrative reforms, education, and open encouragement of new approaches to economic and fiscal policies.

All these measures increased Tafari's popularity, which proved to be a double-edged sword. On the one hand, it confirmed him as the authentic leader of the few young, educated elite and their supporters in the government and emboldened him in his quest for the empire's supreme power, confirming his rightful place in the succession to the Solomonic dynasty. On the other hand, it stoked fear and resentment in Iassu and his supporters. Before his appointment as governor of Harar, Tafari always played by the traditional rule book of protocol, taking care to pay the homage due to Iassu as his political superior, despite his own secret ambitions. It was a delicate situation, involving a game of duplicity, ambiguity, and subterfuge, and Tafari had become a master player by that time, thanks to his own personal experience, particularly at Menelik's court. An example of Tafari's political skills is his response when Iassu, wishing to put him under his control, suggested to Tafari that he marry one of his relatives. Tafari deftly used the language of ambiguity—not refusing, but not exactly accepting the suggestion.

Meanwhile, Iassu's rule (or rather misrule) went from bad to worse. He almost destroyed the central government carefully erected by Menelik, and the imperial court, which under Menelik functioned smoothly, was turned to a hornet's nest in which confusion and uncertainty prevailed. In that chaos, only Harar was stable, as Tafari put into practice revolutionary forms of governance, including improvement in the treatment of peasants, land tenure, and taxation.

Some well-known nobles, led by one Ras Abate, actually planned a coup to overthrow Iassu. But those opposed to the coup were able to thwart it. Empress Taitu was at the center of it, and a member of her camp tried to enlist

Tafari's support. In language that exemplified Tafari's skill, he answered by saying he was too young to get involved in so momentous a scheme: "It is simply over my head." In his memoirs, Ras Imru, who had inklings of Tafari's ambitions, expresses admiration of such uncanny ability.

It was at this time that Taitu appointed Tafari to be governor of Harar, while also suggesting a suitable marriage with one of her relatives. Though the decline in her power was already known, and a plot to oust her was already a foregone conclusion, Tafari paid her a respectful farewell visit before he headed to Harar. In the language of gambling, he hedged all his bets. At the same time, he did not miss an opportunity to demonstrate by example how his mode of rule differed from the disastrous rule of Iassu. One of the serious complaints leveled at Iassu was that he consistently favored the Muslims of the empire, showing complete disregard for the old system of government and especially for the Christian Orthodox Church's teachings. In an interesting contrast, whereas his father, King Michael, was born a Muslim and was converted to Christianity by Emperor Yohannes, Iassu seemed to wish to become a Muslim. Those who defend Iassu's Islamic tendencies claim that he was a visionary who wanted to unite Ethiopia by building a firm bridge between the two religions. If that is a fair assessment of Iassu's vision, it was not accompanied by the requisite need to take into account the stubborn reality of Ethiopia at the time, or the key role of the Christian Orthodox Church in Ethiopian history and politics.

Additionally, Iassu's partiality to the Muslims of Ethiopia was complicated by his partiality to the wrong powers in the World War I conflict, the Germans and Turks, which went against the interests of the European powers that surrounded Ethiopia, the British and the French. In the slowly developing drama pitting the modernizing or "progressive" forces rallying behind Tafari and those of Iassu, the position of the European powers was crucial. Tafari, ever the clever manipulator of forces and events, used his British and French contacts as well as Ethiopians sympathetic to his cause to discredit Iassu's politics of support for the wrong side.

He also expressed his dismay and bitter disappointment at Lij Iassu's continued abuse of the sacred duties of his imperial office, entrusted to him by no less a historic personage than his maternal grandfather, Menelik. A historic denouement was approaching. Lij Iassu was spending more time away from the capital, hunting, wenching, and fraternizing with Muslim leaders in the Danakil plains and elsewhere. In some historical accounts, there is even a hint of his being engaged in slave trading at least once in the southern district of Ghimira, as well as in atrocious behavior such as rape and massacre.[1] Tafari's response is interesting in its subtlety and suggestiveness. He said, "Lij Iassu sought in everything the company and counsel of worthless men who only wanted their immediate profit, while the great nobles and ministers became hostile and removed their hearts from him."[2]

As Tafari's popularity increased, with his supporters openly praising his leadership qualities, the relationship between him and Iassu worsened. This led Tafari's supporters to imagine the worst, including the danger of his being kidnapped by the powerful Ras Mikael, Iassu's father, governor of the Wollo region, where the famous Meqdela fortress with its inaccessible royal prison called Wohni Amba is found. Readers of Samuel Johnson's 1715 novel, *Ras Selas,* will recall that the locus for the novel was the same Wohni Amba, in which princes who were considered potential threats to the reigning monarch were incarcerated. Ras Mikael was so determined to have his son rule Ethiopia that it was feared he would not hesitate to remove his son's potential rivals. During Menelik's last days, his powerful consort, Empress Taitu, had consigned a disgraced Ras Abate to Mikael for imprisonment at Meqdela.[3]

As unrest mounted, Iassu's open defiance of the political reality of Ethiopia and association with Islam provided the conservative Orthodox Christian nobility with a pretext for orchestrating his removal from power. As the reasons for his removal are well established, and the result was the eventual rise of Tafari to become Ethiopia's leader, a few words of reflection on Iassu's vision would be worthwhile.

## Iassu's Vision

There is a yet unanswered oral tradition that challenges the official version of modern Ethiopian history as regards the place of Lij Iassu. The gist of the challenge is that all official history is the "victor's version," written to please the powers that be and to suit their scripted version. Implicit in this oral tradition is a demand for a fairer and more accurate rendering of Iassu's place, which would require a reinterpretation of the reasons for and circumstances of the charge of his apostasy and his alleged Islamic favoritism. As to Iassu's fitness to rule the complex empire-state built so carefully by Menelik, the record supports a judgment that is not favorable to him. Certainly, again on the record, in terms of mental fitness—of sobriety and balance—there is no comparison to Tafari.

However, in the context of a constitutionally guaranteed equality, one wonders whether such a victor's version of history would pass muster today, particularly in view of an aroused Ethiopian Muslim community that contends that the constitutional guarantee of equality extends to all citizens in every respect. Such a challenge inevitably raises issues of the right balance between human rights (including religious rights) on the one hand, and stability of the state on the other. The fear on the part of those who cling to what we may call the officially sanctioned version of history is a genuine fear that their dearly held values would be under threat of being, at the very least, devalued. These are predominantly adherents to the Orthodox Christian faith, to whom the close ties that bind church and state form part of the historical DNA of the Ethiopian state. They feel discomfort from the kind of challenge the Iassu story and his supposed unifying vision implies.

Was Iassu's vision a mirage, or does it contain within it the possibility of reimagining a history in which Christian and Muslim citizens would be made to feel equally secure by a constitutionally guaranteed principle of equality, leaving the actual mutual acceptance and accommodation to be worked out in the crucible of social and political interactions? This is a serious question that all thoughtful citizens of Ethiopia (and of Eritrea) should reflect upon. To that end, the history of the Iassu-Tafari feud provides useful lessons.

# 5

# The 1916 Coup d'État and the Rise of a Man of Destiny

> The same arts that did gain
> A power, must it maintain.
>
> —Andrew Marvell

## Between Two Worlds

The world of Tafari and of his cohort of modernizing supporters was an imagined world of progress pitted against a backward-looking traditional society. The first time the Ethiopian state confronted modern (European) ideas and institutions in a serious way was during the tumultuous reign of Emperor Teodros in the mid-nineteenth century. Teodros was shocked to find that his country was at a disadvantage compared to European countries, notably Britain, with which he corresponded and by which he was later defeated. Teodros strongly believed that Ethiopia needed to emulate Europe and catch up in its material and technical achievements; but he fell short of achieving his goal.

Menelik, who spent his youth at Teodros's court, first as prisoner, then as a favored adopted son, learned a thing or two from him. Much of his policy of what we can call modernization was inspired by Teodros's vision of a united Ethiopia with modern administration and a national army and civil service. Through a combination of good fortune and an expanded and more richly endowed country than Teodros had ruled over, Menelik was able to fulfill some of Teodros's aims. And whereas Teodros dealt harshly with any opposition, including an ultraconservative clergy, Menelik followed a policy of accommodation and compromise. It was because of his wise policies as well as his popularity that Menelik was able to hold a backward church leashed and fearful of crossing him by standing in the way of the progress achieved under his reign, such as it was. But with Menelik incapacitated by a debilitating stroke, the forces of tradition seemed to have a new lease on life, with the backing of powerful feudal lords who were masters of their own domains. Menelik's expanded empire provided many of these lords with profitable land and subject peoples whom they could exploit. In this, the church worked hand in hand with the state as an integral part of the "civilizing mission" in a new imperial enterprise engineered and driven by Menelik and his minions. In that sense, therefore, Menelik is truly the creator of a new and expanded Ethiopia.[1]

It was in this context that the daring idea of modernization imagined by Tafari and his modernizing group of followers was advanced. In the proverbial opposition between an irresistible force and an immovable object, the forces of change led by Tafari were opposed by the forces of reaction, including Menelik's widow, Empress Taitu, and the provincial and feudal lords. The opposed forces represented not only conflicting ideas about modernity and progress but, perhaps more importantly, conflicting interests. It was a power struggle between a reactionary feudal class and an incipient investing bourgeoisie that was small in number but dynamic and forward-looking, with knowledge as its initial capital.

Tafari, standing at the center of that dynamic class, attracted all the young men with a modern education and those among the products of traditional education who had nevertheless seen the advantages of modernization. Two of the best known among the latter were Takele Woldehawariat and Woldegiorgis Woldeyohannes, who would later play key roles in Haile Selassie's government.

## Tafari the Antifeudal Modernizer

It seems a contradiction in terms to characterize as antifeudal a prince like Tafari. The truth is that he was a prince born to a progressively inclined father, Ras Makonnen, who was Menelik's principal point of contact with the world of European ideas and institutions like banking and trade. When Makonnen traveled to Europe, one of the things he did was to open a bank account in Europe. Makonnen appreciated the power of money and the monetized economy, as did Tafari, and they both used the geographical position of Harar and the French-Ethiopian Railway company as the principal entry point for advancing trade and commercial development in Ethiopia. But while Tafari was a prince-entrepreneur who appreciated the power of money and of modern ideas and institutions, he was also keenly aware of the power of the landed gentry and handled them with care until he was in a position to control them through the agency of a centralized modern state. Tafari's conviction of the power of modern ideas and institutions would be further reinforced by his visit to European countries after he was secure as crown prince and chief executive officer following the coup d'état versus Iassu.[2]

During the period of uncertainty, with Tafari's star shining more and more brightly, a fearful Iassu agreed to Tafari's appointment as governor of Harar, presumably hoping to keep him away from the center, where the drama was being played out. Iassu also made Tafari swear an oath of loyalty. With his growing influence, Tafari faced the danger of being kidnapped by King Michael, Iassu's doting father, and imprisoned in Wohni Amba (the dreadful royal prison where former kings had kept potential rivals). The relationship between Iassu and Tafari had deteriorated. In 1915, Iassu traveled to Harar where his close connections with Muslim leaders became evident.

It was also during this period that Tafari nearly drowned in Haremaya (Alemaya) Lake. His former teacher, Aba Samuel, lost his own life in saving him. The suspicion that Iassu had bribed an agent to cause the accident, if true, only shows how desperate he had become about Tafari's growing power and influence. In May 1916, Iassu summoned Tafari to Addis Ababa. This gave Tafari an opportunity to consult with the Shoan power brokers, including the Council of Ministers. In his memoirs, Ras Imru describes how, while Tafari was in Addis Ababa, Iassu, in a last desperate act, traveled to Harar to mobilize his Muslim followers in the province and to distribute arms, preparing them for a final confrontation with Tafari's forces.[3] By September of that year, the forces were aligning, and there was tension in Addis Ababa, as some of Tafari's educated supporters felt their lives to be threatened. Two of these, Paulos Menameno and Aba Petros of the Catholic mission in Dire Dawa, happened to visit Harar, where they warned Ras Imru to take cautionary measures.[4]

According to Ras Imru's account, in addition to mobilizing and arming Muslim forces, Iassu also gave a banquet to prominent members of the Christian gentry, including veteran statesman Dejasmach Balcha, and gave a speech accusing Tafari of conspiring against him. In a dramatic exchange of words, Iassu was told in no uncertain terms that it was he who was conspiring against the state by consorting with Islam forces. Iassu denied the charge and, putting his hand on the Bible, swore an oath of loyalty to the Christian faith before a disbelieving audience.

Soon thereafter, Iassu removed Dejasmach Tafari from his governorship of Harar, and at the same time ordered an invasion of his Harar residence. This act provided Tafari a reason to release himself from the oath of loyalty, thus allowing himself to take a leading role in the 1916 coup.

### The Coup d'État

Aware of Tafari's influence, the Shoan power brokers, headed by Fitawrari Habtegiorgis, had extracted a promise from him not to seek the throne. On February 11, 1917, they decided to depose Iassu and appoint Menelik's daughter, Zewditu, empress, with Tafari as chief executive and heir to the throne and Habtegiorgis as minister of war. This gave rise to what historians of the period have called a triumvirate, though Zewditu was a "sleeping partner," overwhelmed by Tafari's dynamic power.

Iassu was deposed but not finished; he escaped capture and headed to the Danakil plains, where he felt safe among people he considered loyal Muslim devotees. He was eventually captured, and died in prison in 1936. The Iassu-Tafari saga was finally settled in October 1916 at the battle of Sagalaye, in which the forces of Iassu's father, King Michael, were defeated by Tafari's forces. In sum, there were three factors that caused Iassu's fall. First was his dismissal of Tafari from his Harar governorship, which provoked a hostile reaction from Tafari's loyalists. Secondly, his alliance with the Germans and Turks in the 1914–18 war aroused the anger of the British and the French, pushing them to Tafari's side. Thirdly, his dalliance with Muslim leaders and appearance of abandoning the Christian faith alienated the powerful Christian establishment. The patriarch publicly proclaimed an act of excommunication, releasing all concerned from the oath of loyalty they had sworn in accordance with Emperor Menelik's demands upon designating his grandson, Iassu, to succeed him.

Conflicts arose within the triumvirate, which inevitably led to plots and counterplots. In one such conspiracy, the Council of Ministers, presumably under Habtegiorgis's urging, proposed to rein in Tafari's power, which Tafari vigorously resisted. In the power struggle, Tafari's loyalists everywhere showed superior organization and determination. In a showdown at the Jan-Meda plains, Tafari's forces were able to literally shout down the opponents and secure the support of a majority of the power brokers, thus defeating the conspiracy.

To confirm his freshly gained executive power, Tafari was able to banish all members of the Council of Ministers, except Habtegiorgis, to their respective provinces. Tafari learned a great lesson from all this plotting and counterplotting. It was probably at that time that a popular verse was composed:

Harar'n babatu shoa'n begulbetu
Wollo'n begabcha
Ingdih Man Alla, Teqil ante b'cha!

(He got Harar through his father. He got Shoa by dint of force, and Wollo through marriage. Now who else is there except you—O Teqil!)[5]

## A Man of Destiny

Throughout the time of bitter conflict that ended in his favor, what distinguished Tafari Makonnen (soon to be renamed Haile Selassie) was his clear vision for his country, a vision defined by his acute sense of the need for his country to adopt modern ideas and methods in order to join the family of civilized nations. While Menelik entertained similar sentiments, Tafari had to fight for them tooth and nail, nearly losing his life in the attempt. His toughness and determination as well as his unique political skills equipped him for the enormous task, involving some serious conflict with an old established system. But as the title of chapter 2, "Orphaned Prince Steeled by Adversity," suggests, a deep desire to attain the supreme power of the state must have been conditioned by deeper psychological factors having to do with losing a nurturing mother and having a frequently absent father who also died when he was still young. One can doubtless cite other examples of historical figures whose single-minded quest for certain things in life (such as power) was conditioned by similar experiences.

One example will suffice to distinguish Tafari from another great Ethiopian historical figure, Habtegiorgis, with whom he was involved in a tug-of-war during much of the triumvirate period. Tafari's quiet mode of operation, which masked an iron will and guile, enabled him to persuade his foes to relent, particularly in his dogged struggle to end slavery. The issue of slavery came to the fore when, in 1923, Tafari vigorously advocated that Ethiopia should apply for admission to the League of Nations. There was opposition within the league to Ethiopia, as a state that permitted slavery, being allowed to join, as well as tremendous opposition from conservatives within Ethiopia, most of whom owned slaves. Tafari was able to persuade some of the most influential men, such as Habtegiorgis, that membership in the League of Nations would be good for Ethiopia's security, and convince the most important provincial governors to back a proclamation to abolish slavery. Considering the conditions of the time, this was no mean achievement, for slavery was part of the socioeconomic fabric of society. To put it succinctly, the abolition of slavery meant the liberation of a mass of humanity that was chained to the feudal lords and their hangers-on. It would mean the end of the privileges of feudal lords and their eventual impoverishment. Their resistance would make Tafari's task enormous, if not impossible. That slavery was not ended (indeed could not be ended) then is a function of the hard reality the emperor was up against. It had to wait until another day. But the war against slavery (and slaveholders) had been declared.

Tafari's next bold stroke occurred in 1924, when he proposed to go on an extended tour of Europe, and to take along a number of the figures who were posing a threat to him at the time, including the provincial governors Ras Hailu of Gojam and Ras Seyoum of Tigray. Including them was a risky and delicate task, as he explains in his autobiography.[6] Before Tafari, no Ethiopian head of state had ever ventured out of the country. Prior to the European visit in 1924, he had traveled to the then British possession of Aden.

Before reaching Europe, Tafari visited Cairo and Jerusalem, then proceeded to Marseilles, Rome, Paris, and London. During his four and a half months of travel, he visited educational institutions as well as government and commercial enterprises and industrial plants, while Ras Hailu and Ras Seyoum and other members of his entourage went on a sightseeing and shopping spree. Tafari set out to turn his diplomatic tour de force into a propaganda weapon that would change the minds of the conservative opponents of progress. For example, once the Rases and their kind got used to such products of industrial civilization as cars, they would be more inclined to accept the idea of progress in general. Cars needed roads, and building roads would mean the building of further infrastructure. It would be the beginning of a long process of development.

Tafari knew, of course, that at the heart of all development lay education. Therefore, immediately after his European tour he opened a school, the Tafari Makonnen

School, with his own money and sent for teachers to be brought there. At the opening ceremony of the school, Tafari harangued the conservative assembly of Rases and others who had been dragooned to attend. "The time has passed for mere lip-service to our country," he said. "The crying need of our people is education, without which we cannot maintain our independence. The proof of real patriotism is to recognize this fact and—in the case of those who possess the means—to found schools and to forward the cause of education in every way. I have built this school as a beginning and as an example, which I appeal to the wealthy among the people to follow."[7]

Commenting on Tafari's speech and initiative, British traveler Charles F. Rey presciently wrote, "If it succeeds and extends [it] may affect profoundly the future of the country. It is of course for this reason that it was opposed by the reactionary elements." When the school opened in 1926, it had places for 180 children, bringing the total of places available at the time in the whole of Ethiopia to 291.[8]

In view of these simple facts, it is not difficult to imagine the scale of the effort and resources it would take to advance the education of Ethiopians to fulfill the developmental needs of the country. Any leader in his place, whether a king or president, would have had his work cut out for him; it was not an enviable position to be in. Yet Tafari then, and later as Haile Selassie, was not awed by the enormity of the challenge. Indeed, he seems to have thrived on meeting it.

The resistance to change that was the cause of so much conflict in the governing triumvirate slowly gave way to reluctant acceptance. When Habtegiorgis died in 1926, Tafari was left to deal with the aging and gradually weakening Empress Zewditu. Not long after Habtegiorgis's death, the empress, presumably at the behest of some ambitious chiefs in her court, tried to overthrow Tafari in what became known as the Aba Wukaw incident. Aba Wukaw was out to arrest Tafari in his palace in the name of the empress on the grounds that Tafari was undermining her authority and usurping her power. Aba Wukaw failed and was brought in chains before Tafari, where the assembled noblemen (whose actions were less than noble) recommended that he be hanged for his crime. Tafari spared his life but sent him to prison. The occasion provided Tafari's supporters a golden opportunity to force the empress to name Tafari king, a title that in a traditional society such as this one would significantly enhance his authority. Never one to miss an occasion warranting publicity, Tafari ordered that his coronation be attended by envoys of foreign powers, especially those with colonies around Ethiopia. Accordingly, preparations were planned for a grand ceremony. But a ceremony on an even grander scale was to take place soon, to which governments of almost all of Europe would be invited to send their envoys. That occasion was the coronation of Tafari as emperor upon the death of Empress Zewditu.

6

# From King to Emperor

## *Proclamation of the Central Elements of Change*

In early April 1930, two years after she was forced to crown Tafari king, Zewditu died. Hers is a sad tale of an unfortunate princess who was a prisoner of circumstance, caught in the middle of a power play among ruthless people, her position making her the object of their ambitious schemes. These people included Menelik's widow, the redoubtable Empress Taitu, who wedded Zewditu to her nephew, Ras Gugsa, a northern warlord. All her life the unfortunate woman had been a target for ambitious men who sought to marry her by hook or crook. One such was Ras Abate, who made an unsuccessful attempt to invade the palace and kidnap her. Had he succeeded, their marriage would have been a fait accompli, according to the traditional Ethiopian practice of *tilfia* (elopement). He failed miserably.

Gugsa was still married to Zewditu when the Shoan men of power elevated her to her father's throne, replacing Iassu. For reasons of state, these men prevented Gugsa from becoming consort. Tafari in particular feared Gugsa's influence as a threat to his own plans. This was one of the many examples in which the mild-mannered Tafari showed his iron will and ruthlessness. He simply forbade the empress to see her husband, announcing to her that henceforth she was divorced from him. She had no choice but to resign herself to her fate as a pawn in the merciless intrigue of palace politics. Zewditu apparently loved Ras Gugsa and did not forgive Tafari for denying her the love and comfort of her husband. Love, in this case, did not conquer all, contrary to the old adage *amor omnia vincit!*

The frustrated Gugsa rebelled, raising a northern army and posing a serious threat to Tafari's position and even the unity of the country. The full fury of the Shoan armed forces was brought upon him, including the use of air power for the first time in Ethiopia as a weapon of war. He was defeated and killed, and it was the news of her husband's death that dealt the coup de grâce to the ailing empress.

Immediately upon Zewditu's death, Tafari issued a proclamation informing the Ethiopian public of her death and his succession to the throne as emperor under the name of Haile Selassie. The substantial part of the proclamation reads as follows:

> PROCLAMATION . . . In accordance with the Proclamation which our Creator abiding in His people, and electing us, did cause to be made, we have lived without breach of our Covenant as mother and son.

> Now, in that by law and commandment of God, none that is human may avoid return to earth, Her Majesty the Empress, after a few days of sickness, has departed this life. The passing of Her Majesty the Empress is grievous for myself and for the whole of the Empire. Since it is the long-standing custom that when a King, the Shepherd of his people, shall die, a King replaces him, I being upon the seat of David to which I was betrothed, will, by God's charity, watch over you.
>
> Trader, trade! Farmer plough! I shall govern you by the law and ordinance that has come to me, handed down from fathers.[1]

The sentiment that the death of the empress was grievous for him shows hypocrisy in the service of "reasons of state," for in view of the decade-long struggle that preceded her death, no one could have been happier than he at her passing.

So, under the name of Haile Selassie, King Tafari, at the age of thirty-seven, became emperor of Ethiopia.[2] He decided to make his coronation a memorable occasion, one that would add value to his diplomacy and domestic politics. He wanted to send a clear signal to the international community, especially European powers, as well as impress upon Ethiopians the principal objectives of his vision, stressing the dire need for education and for the introduction of centralized administration as the backbone of unity and peaceful development.

## Central Elements of the Required Change

Haile Selassie did not waste time in reordering his priorities and reorganizing his principal supporters. He made it abundantly clear to all concerned, especially his band of followers, that the first agenda was clipping the wings of the provincial potentates, the Rases, and bringing them under the control of a centralized state effectively controlled by him and a select cadre of modern-minded people. Next, he repeatedly mentioned education as a necessary instrument of modernization as well as a culture-enhancing force, and thus of great value in and of itself. This he had always emphasized by taking initiative and spending his own money to establish educational institutions. The rest of his program, such as economic development, including building infrastructure, would follow suit inevitably. Additionally, and no less important, social issues, including the need to create a regime of equality as a fundamental basis of peace and social solidarity, would have to be guaranteed under a new constitutional dispensation. Emperor Haile Selassie showed once again his considerable political skills in planning and organizing his coronation. First of all he secured the services of the few educated Ethiopians in the planning. Principal among these was Fitawrari Teklehawariat, a protégé of Ras Makonnen, who had studied military science in Russia, sent there by Ras Makonnen with Menelik's blessing. He had also spent time in France studying agricultural science.

The emperor summoned all the Rases to Addis Ababa to attend the coronation, and subsequently kept them as hostages for a whole year until he was ready to spring on them the most important instrument of his modernizing scheme.[3] In 1931, one year after his coronation, he announced that a modern constitution had been drafted that would be the basis of his government, including the government in the provinces. Modeled on a number of foreign constitutions, including that of Japan, it was drafted by a committee in which Teklehawariat played a key role. He was also given the privilege of reading and explaining its basic features to an assembly of all the most important personalities of the empire, including the Rases and their associates in the capital. Teklehawariat was eloquent and bold in explaining the basic features of the constitution.

In his speech delivered at the signing of the constitution, the emperor affirmed that it would mark a transformation of Ethiopia into a limited monarchy, "whereby the whole people may be made to share our labors in accomplishing the heavy task of government at which former Emperors labored alone." To those ends, the constitution introduced two deliberative chambers—a senate, appointed by the emperor, and a chamber of deputies, chosen by dignitaries and chiefs to advise the emperor. The members would come from the various provinces, chosen under the authority of the emperor "until such time as the people have reached a degree of education and experience enabling them to make the choice themselves. . . . Decisions taken in parliament and approved by the Emperor will be executed for the whole of Ethiopia and by Ministers."[4]

This, for the time, was indeed revolutionary.

Many commentators in Europe sneered at all this, calling it "window dressing," while a few well-wishers thought it a brave first step from feudalism toward democracy. Time would tell which of these views was well founded. But in its objectives, it was a blow for change, striking at the root of the powers and privileges of all potentates on three issues: security, taxation, and local administration.

With respect to security, henceforth there would be a salaried national army under the control of the central government. The Rases would no longer have the right to keep a private provincial army that could threaten or undermine the central government. Needless to say, this was a blow to the power of the Rases. With respect to taxation, all taxable income would be regulated by law issued by the central government; all regional potentates, from the Rases down to their local agents at the village level, were thus denied the financial basis of their feudal power. With regard to local administration, the plan was to send central government–appointed personnel to the regions and their local administrative units. For the first phase of the scheme, however, the governors would be chosen from loyal members of the old guard. The full implementation of the administrative reform would begin after the restoration in 1941, as we shall see in a later chapter.

By 1932, the emperor had established the principle of central government as a central guiding concept and forced the Rases to accept it. What remained was to apply it in fact, not just in theory. That would come in time. What counted now was that he had assumed supreme power, having vanquished all his adversaries. Among the diehard feudal lords, the Tigrean lords and Ras Hailu of Gojam, who had been kept in Addis Ababa since the coronation as "honored guests" of the emperor, had no choice but to accept the idea of central rule as defined in the constitution. The emperor had seen to it that the Rases were involved in discussions on the draft constitution. In one of his speeches, he said he wanted to promulgate a constitution "to bequeath to our heirs a rule that is based on law to bring our people into partnership in the work of government."[5]

It was probably at this time that the place of his birth, Ejersa Goro, was renamed Bet-Lehem. I have found no written evidence of who was responsible for deciding to name it after the place where Jesus Christ was born; perhaps some ecclesiastic true believers, assisted by imperial bureaucrats, were carried away by their fanatical enthusiasm. But it was obviously another aspect of the attempt to connect him to Christ. There is no record of whether the emperor encouraged the renaming of Ejersa Goro; nor is there evidence that he discouraged it. Nor did he take any steps to discourage the Rastafarians in Jamaica from adopting him as their God. Indeed, he made land grants to some of their members in southern Ethiopia, at a place called Shashemenne.

# 7

# The Italian Invasion and the Emperor's Exile

The memory of Ethiopia's crushing victory over the Italian forces at Adua in 1896 haunted the successive leaders of Italy. Among these, none was more adamant in seeking to avenge the humiliating defeat than the Fascist leader Benito Mussolini. He had signed a Treaty of Friendship with Ethiopia in 1928, but would use it only as a wedge to invade Ethiopia later. While Emperor Haile Selassie put his trust in the treaty, just as he did in the Covenant of the League of Nations, European powers dismissed such trust as naïveté, aware of Italy's interest in making Ethiopia at best a client state beholden to Italy, and at worst a future colony. As it turned out, the European powers were right: Mussolini was secretly planning a military attack on Ethiopia, using the defeat at Adua as a pretext to arouse Italian public opinion in support of his project. In secret correspondence between Mussolini and General De Bono, his close military advisor, the general wrote,

> The political conditions in Abyssinia [Ethiopia] are deplorable; it should not be a very difficult task to effect

> the disintegration of the Empire if we work at it well on political lines, and it could be regarded as certain after a military victory on our part. . . . [I]t is incumbent on us to prepare ourselves, so that we could withstand the shock of the whole Abyssinian force in our present position and then pass to the counter-attack, and go right in with the intention of making a complete job of it, once and for all.[1]

The diplomatic history of the Italo-Ethiopian war of 1936 is a sordid story of duplicity and betrayal in which Emperor Haile Selassie made the mistake (as some have argued) of placing undue trust in international treaties and the notion of collective security guaranteed under such treaties. Whether Italy's motive in invading Ethiopia was to avenge the "shame of Adua" or to further her territorial expansion, the League of Nations' betrayal of Ethiopia is one of the twentieth century's tragic episodes. But it also elevated Haile Selassie into an important figure in international affairs, as the embodiment of victimhood and the rights of small nations. His Geneva speech to the League of Nations was a stern rebuke to the world powers for their betrayal of international law and morality in failing to live up to their treaty obligations to sanction an aggressor and come to the defense of the nation it invaded. As presented in the media, his appearance in Geneva, draped in a royal Ethiopian cape, his gentle manner and attractive persona, and above all his historic speech rebuking the world powers, telling them that God and history would be their judge, impressed itself on the psyche of a troubled world at a time when Hitler in Germany was posing a clear challenge to Britain and France. Most thoughtful people in Europe saw Haile Selassie as a symbol of a troubled world in which the dark cloud of war was looming on the horizon.

Having failed to move the League of Nations, Haile Selassie settled in Bath, England, where he began a five-year exile that would last until the start of the Second World War. Throughout that sad episode, a few devoted supporters in England never stopped espousing Ethiopia's cause as represented by the emperor. Among them, the indefatigable and indomitable Sylvia Pankhurst figured prominently, ceaselessly writing and lobbying members of the British Parliament.[2]

By some accounts, the emperor faced financial difficulties and may have undergone depression during the earlier part of his exile. For someone who had been busy all his life ruling over people, making decisions that affected the lives and deaths of thousands, it must have been hard to be without work, at the head of a family that faced, if not penury, certainly great discomfort. In his autobiography, he says that when he left his country he had a fervent hope that the League of Nations would help him recover his lost kingdom. How bitter he must have been to realize that the provisions of the League's charter were no more than empty words. Due to his misplaced trust in the League and in "collective security," he says, he was not able to take much with him when he left his country. And what he had, he shared with some needy exiles among his close kinsmen. Despite the generosity of some individuals in England, therefore, he was left mostly to his own devices. It was during this depressing period that he chose not to address the Council of the League, dispatching, in his place, the loyal and ever-optimistic Dr. Lorenzo Taezaz. All to no avail.

During these hard times, he was also faced with a cruel choice. The Italian government offered to let him return if he would accept a reduced status and acknowledge their sovereignty. Many among the Ethiopian nobility, including Rases, had been bribed to denounce him and recognize the Italian occupation. Only Ras Imru, true to his character, rejected the blandishments of Mussolini and his minions with the contempt they deserved and refused to denounce his royal cousin and sovereign. He spent five miserable years in an Italian island prison, mocked by his jailors but honored and hailed by his compatriots. Upon Haile Selassie's return to his throne, one of his first actions was to inquire into Imru's whereabouts. His British allies traced Imru and brought him back to his country, where a tearful reunion took place between the two cousins and comrades when Imru arrived at the Addis Ababa airport. This was the only occasion when the protocol-conscious Haile Selassie went to the airport to greet a fellow Ethiopian, exhibiting a rarely expressed emotional side of him.

During the five bitter years of exile, the emperor stayed in contact with the *arbegnas*, the guerrilla fighters in Ethiopia, who saw to it that the occupation would not be a bed of roses for the Italians. The heroic acts of the guerrillas kept alive, for the emperor and all the other exiles, the hope of eventual liberation. Led by Abebe Aregai (who would be promoted to Ras following liberation) in the central region of Shoa and by prominent people like Takele Woldehawariat and Amoraw Wubneh in the Gondar region in the northwest, the guerrillas continually harassed the occupying regime. While some Ethiopians defected to the enemy and acted as collaborators, others, under the guise of working with the Italians, gathered needed information for the guerrillas

It is worth noting that several units of Eritreans who had been part of the invading Italian forces defected to join their Ethiopian brothers to fight the common enemy. Two notable figures are Abraha Deboch and Mogues Asgedom. One day in February 1937, these young Eritreans, who were in the employ of the Italian government in Addis Ababa, made an attempt on the life of Marshal Graziani, the Fascist governor of Ethiopia, throwing a bomb at him while he was addressing a public meeting. He was badly wounded but survived. In a recent book, *The Plot to Kill Graziani*, Ian Campbell has unearthed some intriguing details about Deboch and Asgedom.[3] They were betrayed by Ethiopian residents of the Wolkait region of Gondar and handed over to the Italian rulers, who executed them; their remains were later unearthed and reburied at the cemetery of the Church of Qidiste Selassie (Holy Trinity Church), an honor reserved for patriots and heroes of the war. Incidentally, Lorenzo Taezaz was also buried in the same cemetery, as was Sylvia Pankhurst, in recognition of her service to Ethiopia during the hard times.

# 8

# World War II and the Return of the Emperor to Ethiopia

It was as if his words had been fulfilled—the words of the tragic figure who, standing on the podium of the League of Nations in 1936, warned the members that God and history would judge them. When war broke out in 1939, with Mussolini's Italy siding with Hitler's Germany, Haile Selassie instantly became a prophet among thoughtful people, particularly in Britain. For people in the African Diaspora, particularly in the United States and the Caribbean region, his name became a talisman for Africa's liberation. And it did not take long for the leaders of the British government to call on him, telling him to get ready—it was time to go back home! This, from those who wouldn't touch "the little man" with a ten-foot pole during his bitter days of exile.

Italy occupied Ethiopia for five years. At the very beginning of the occupation, the Italian government announced the creation of an Italian Eastern Africa (*Africa Orientale Italiana*), joining Eritrea, Ethiopia and Somalia. With the declaration of war, the entire territory would become part of the African theater of war when the Allied troops attacked all Italian possessions, including Libya in North Africa. It was as a part of that war effort that the British government under Winston Churchill called on Haile Selassie to proceed to Sudan, from which he would go back to his occupied country to dislodge the Italians. He had been well aware of the state of his country, having sent Lorenzo Taezaz to test the mood of his people. Lorenzo, a brilliant Eritrean-born doctor of law, was the principal draftsman of the emperor's famous Geneva speech, and also read his second address to the League when the emperor could not attend due to illness. As the emperor's special emissary, he had trekked through Gojam and Gondar in 1938 and 1939, openly telling people to rise up for liberation.

Haile Selassie traveled to Khartoum via Egypt accompanied by a British journalist, his son, Makonnen, and his two principal aides, Lorenzo and Woldegiorgis Woldeyohannes. Following months of delay caused by the reluctance of the British military high command to assist the emperor in his desire to enter Ethiopia at the head of his patriotic forces, the emperor crossed the border from Sudan on January 20, 1941. His forces were commanded by Major Orde Wingate, a British officer with a messianic sense of his cause who saw the emperor as a David facing the Italian Goliath. So, after five years of painful exile, Emperor Haile Selassie landed on the soil of his country and raised the red, green, and gold standard with the Lion of Judah inset to flutter in the light breeze. In his speech, delivered in Amharic, the emperor thanked the British public, saying, "Before I go I would like to say that I shall never forget the sympathetic feelings which the British public have shown me in my hours of painful tribulation. I understand, and I am grateful to them."[1]

The journey was hard, testing even a hardy soldier like Wingate, but the Ethiopian patriotic forces fought their way to Debra Marcos, the capital of Gojam, on April 4, 1941. Two days later, the emperor accepted the surrender of Ras Hailu, Gojam's governor, who had collaborated with the invaders. Haile Selassie forgave Ras Hailu, but kept him under close surveillance for the rest of his life.

The duplicity and ulterior motives of the British government at the time are evident in an exchange at this point between Wingate and the high command. Wingate, a true believer in Ethiopia's total liberation and the restoration of its sovereign to his throne, was known for his defiance of orders when they conflicted with his sense of right. When he received a radio message from Khartoum informing him that the South African armed forces under General Cunningham were about to enter Addis Ababa and he was to halt all operations and keep the emperor at Debra Marcos, Wingate's response was to request that a plane be sent immediately so that the emperor could be flown to his capital and receive the homage and welcome of his people. The high command refused the request and sternly ordered Wingate to keep the emperor where he was. The reason they gave was that there were over twenty-five thousand Italians in Addis Ababa—white people, for heaven's sake! "If the Emperor arrives, the natives will panic. They will go wild and start looting and raping, and the Italians will all be killed. *So keep the little man out*" (my italics).[2]

The high command's order was repeated by General Cunningham, who told Wingate to halt by "everything short of force" any attempt of the emperor to approach Addis Ababa. Neither Wingate nor the emperor was in any mood to be dissuaded from entering Addis Ababa, and so the emperor entered his capital on May 5, 1941. He stopped at the Dabra-Libanos Church and also at the Entoto Church of Saint Mary to offer prayers of thanks, after which his procession formed for a triumphal entry to his capital. They entered with Wingate seated on a white horse and Haile Selassie in the back seat of an Alfa Romeo taken from Ras Hailu in Debra Marcos. Surely one cannot imagine a more poignant sense of the irony of history and poetic justice.

The emperor waxed eloquent in his speech.

> On this day, which men of earth and angels of heaven could neither have foreseen nor known, I owe thanks unutterable by the mouth of man to the loving God who has enabled me to be present among you. Today is the beginning of a new era in the history of Ethiopia. . . . Since this is so, do not reward evil for evil. Do not

> commit any act of cruelty like those which the enemy committed against us up to this present time. Do not allow the enemy any occasion to foul the good name of Ethiopia. We shall take his weapons and make him return by the way he came.[3]

A journalist who was present reported that the emperor told him, referring to his speech, "Vraiment, j'ai été très émotionné" (I was really overcome with emotion). The same journalist, who wrote a book on the whole experience, reported that the emperor's speech was received with joy, and that the public left quietly and peacefully "to celebrate but not to loot." He added, "It was just five years to the day since Marshal Badoglio and the Italian Army had marched into Addis Ababa."[4]

# 9

# Postliberation Developments

In his speech, Emperor Haile Selassie spoke of a new era in Ethiopian history. *Addis Zaman* (New era), the leading Amharic daily newspaper, was named in commemoration of the country's newfound freedom and to give institutional expression to the symbolism of liberation articulated by the emperor.

However, the emperor was not able immediately to exercise the sovereignty implicit in his country's newfound freedom. His British war allies, or rather a segment of their government officials, including the military high command in Africa, raised legalistic arguments against full sovereignty. The emperor fought them tooth and nail and, with the help of such figures as Anthony Eden and Churchill, was able to overcome. With the signing of the Anglo-Ethiopian Agreement on January 31, 1942, Ethiopia regained full sovereignty; the two nations signed a renegotiated agreement on December 19, 1944. Opposition remained to Ethiopia joining the United Nations until the peace treaty with Italy was signed. But Emperor Haile Selassie fought hard, and in 1945 Ethiopia became one of the UN's charter members. Ethiopia also signed the Peace Treaty along with the United States, Britain, France, and the other Allied nations.

The Italians had left behind an impressive infrastructure and fledgling industrial and commercial enterprises, and the emperor lost no time in exploiting these legacies to his benefit and to that of his loyal followers. At the same time, he set about organizing his government, forming a cabinet of twelve ministers, of which the political ministries were those of the Interior, Defense, Justice, and Foreign Affairs. The emperor himself held the portfolio for the Ministry of Education, which he held for many years, based on his conviction that education is the key to all other aspects of development.

## Back to the Imperative of Centralized Administration

As already mentioned, Emperor Haile Selassie and his followers placed a premium on centralized administration as the backbone of Ethiopia's peaceful development. For that reason, the centerpiece of the new government became the Ministry of the Interior, and for its minister the emperor chose a man whose competence and loyalty to him were beyond question: Woldegiorgis Woldeyohannes, who, since the mid-1920s, had been prominent among his followers and whose value was based on what one writer has called a "nobility of merit," as opposed to the nobility of privilege enjoyed by feudal lords and their hangers-on.[1] When the emperor (still named Tafari at the time) first noticed Woldegiorgis's bright competence and his command of French, he asked him, as it was his wont, "M'n innarghilih?" (What can we do for you"). He eventually appointed him his private secretary and interpreter, and the emperor's appreciation of his qualities is demonstrated by the fact that Woldegiorgis was among the select chosen few to go into exile with him, where he remained the emperor's loyal aide throughout the years of exile in England.

The work Woldegiorgis accomplished as minister of the interior, particularly the administrative structure of the new regional government administration, envisaged in a law proclaimed in 1943, shows an active and creative mind at work laying down the basic framework of a new centralized administration to replace the outmoded and oppressive feudal structure. In that structure, the center was the Ministry of the Interior, from which a new educated and modern-minded cadre, mostly young, was dispatched to mind the store, so to speak, as directors. The directors were supervised by an older provincial governor whose authority was mostly ceremonial, though handled with care by the modern faction appointed to do the work. The directors reported directly to the minister, who reported to the emperor on essential matters concerning controversial issues. Otherwise the minister was given complete authority on how to run his ministry and oversee the work of the provincial personnel.

Woldegiorgis was also minister of the pen, that is to say, principal secretary to the emperor and custodian of the imperial seal. At one time he also acted as minister of justice. For fourteen years, until his fall in 1955, his power was thus second only to that of the emperor. All people who worked with Woldegiorgis attest to his competence, analytical skills, hard work, and loyalty and generosity to all his subordinates.

Woldegiorgis's commitment to the cause of modern, progressive administration was evident as early as the 1930s, just before the Italian invasion. A journalist who visited Ethiopia at the time quoted him as saying that "we of the younger generation, are the friends of progress and humanism, while they [the Rases] are its enemies! And we do not want to work in vain."[2]

An organizational genius, Woldegiorgis also made sure that young educated people were placed in key positions in all the important ministries, including the position of secretary-general of the ministry. The function of a secretary-general included receiving and filing incoming correspondence and stamping and dispatching outgoing correspondence, which made him the overall supervisor of the ministry's archives; as instruments in the control of the flow of information, the secretaries-general marked the ubiquitous presence of Woldegiorgis, as this author personally witnessed. The position of secretary-general finally came into disuse with the arrival of the computer age.

### Other Parts of the Central Elements of Change

Next to central administration, or rather as a complementary part of it, Emperor Haile Selassie's modernizing project included creating a national army and police force, as well as rationalizing the taxation system—which necessarily included taking away taxing powers from the Rases and their hangers-on in the provinces. Not only was this necessary to relieve the citizens of onerous tax burdens exacted by an avaricious local gentry, but it established a system that would ensure a steady income to the central government, regulated by law and overseen by the Ministry of Finance.

### The Revised Constitution of 1955

Fourteen years after liberation, on the jubilee anniversary of his coronation as emperor, Haile Selassie proclaimed a revised constitution. Apart from greater length, the 1955 constitution rests on a seemingly more modern foundation, both in form and substance, than the 1931 constitution. It has been described as a blueprint for the modernization of the Ethiopian state, particularly in respect of its promise to give the people equal rights under the law, which answers the question about the place of the rule of law in the country. Additionally, as if to answer the question of the people's sharing of sovereignty—an essential feature of the notion of modernity—the constitution also promised the vote to the public. Thus, whereas in the

1931 constitution the members of both chambers were not elected by the people, under the revised constitution, the members of the Chamber of Deputies (the Lower House) were to be elected by the people in a universal suffrage to be defined in an election law.

But the constitution's implementation was delayed, diminishing the promises of democracy and the rule of law, and the result in the end was a denial of the promise of democracy. The band of young educated Ethiopians who were the nucleus of his modernizing policies apparently did not imagine that their leader and idol, the progressive, antifeudal Tafari, would break that promise. Indeed, the fact that one-third of the articles of the constitution dealt with the monarchy and the emperor's traditional powers and privileges, intimating that the position of the emperor was central, undermined the possibility of the installation of a regime of democracy and rule of law in the foreseeable future. It must also be remembered that since the person of the emperor was declared to be sacred, his dignity inviolable, and his power indisputable, one could not imagine any minister defying the emperor, including the pliable prime minister, who served him to his last days, protesting that he had no power.[3]

The emperor retained control over the army and foreign affairs, the power to introduce legislation, and supreme executive power, which he grudgingly shared with his prime minister and ministers under his close and strict supervision. Given that centralization was imperative if the power of the feudal lords was to be destroyed, the emperor's extensive power as both head of state and chief executive was a matter of necessity. In that sense, he was a crucial part of the modernizing project. However, his declared ambition of gradually introducing democracy and a regime based on the rule of law was denied by the constitution's codifying the power and dignity of the emperor, sanctioned by his anointing as well as by tradition. All in all, in the judgment of all close observers and based on the emperor's words and acts, Haile Selassie remained an absolute monarch with absolute power. Whether he was corrupted by such power is a matter of judgment that I will reserve for final assessment at the end of this book.

**The Codes of Law**

As I have noted elsewhere, Emperor Haile Selassie liked to compare himself to the Roman emperor Justinian, who codified Roman law. He considered his revised constitution and the codes of law he promulgated in the late 1950s and early 1960s his prime achievements, and did not take kindly to criticism of them.[4] The most significant codes of law were a Civil Code, drafted by a noted French professor of law, René David; a Penal Code, drafted by a noted Swiss professor of law, Jean Gravin; a Commercial Code; a Maritime Code; and Codes of Civil and Criminal Procedure.

Based on modern systems of law and drafted by some of the best legal minds in the world, but imposed on a traditional society and a semifeudal polity with a modernizing but absolute monarch at the helm, these laws, especially the Civil Code, were the subject of much controversy, as can be imagined. Having been one of those entrusted with the application of some of their provision, I can attest to the immense tension involved in their application and the administration of justice in general, which presented quite a challenge, at times approaching a nightmare. An example of such challenge concerns the age of marriage under the Civil Code compared with the law in traditional systems.

In the original draft of the Civil Code, René David had proposed that the minimum age of marriage be eighteen. When the draft was submitted to the Senate, the older members of that chamber raised a horrific row. Eighteen? Why, the girl will be an old maid! Some of the more enlightened members suggested reducing the age to sixteen. Not acceptable; too old, cried the more traditionally minded. The Senate thus arrived at a deadlock.

What to do?

The draftsman of the Code took the matter to the final arbiter, namely His Imperial Majesty the emperor. Employing the well-known Gallic logic and eloquence, Professor David implored the emperor in the name of progress and historical responsibility to resolve this impasse. Future generations of Ethiopian women will bless you, Sire! Moved, the emperor suggested fifteen as the minimum age. Thus ended the controversy, and the old guard swallowed their pride. To them even fifteen was too old, but they had no option but to accept the imperial judgment. From the perspective of social progress, the law had the effect of protecting young girls from being forced into childhood marriages, which interfered with their education. This was only one of many examples of the tension between the new laws and the old system and old attitudes which died hard.

## The Emperor and the Administration of Justice

One of the precepts of the rule of law is the administration of justice by independent judges who decide cases without fear or favor. Again, I draw from the experience I was privileged to have in the matter of the emperor's role as final judge, which by tradition he was entitled to be. His *Chilot,* or final emperor's court, was held daily to hear appeals from any lower court. Citizens had a constitutional right to petition the emperor, and so no one could stop them from applying to the *Chilot.* All serious commentators on this practice agree that it had more political than judicial value. It was also a way for the emperor to stay in touch with his ordinary subjects, and thousands flocked to the palace to petition him. Only a change in the constitution could provide a solution to that judicial anomaly.

## The Emperor and Economic Development

Ethiopia's economy was and is primarily based on agriculture, which is the mainstay of the lives of the people. Much of farming is dependent on rain, and the failure of rain, followed by drought, has led to periodic famines, including the one that ended the emperor's rule in 1974. This raises the question of what can be done. Is industrialization the answer, the way out of the cycle of famine caused by drought? Well, it is part of the answer, but industrialization is a long process, one that depends on surpluses provided from agriculture. So we have a vicious circle.

Emperor Haile Selassie had been in the forefront, acting as example and source of inspiration in investment in private enterprise, beginning from his days in Harar as prince-entrepreneur. Such encouragement was not limited to his considerable private enterprise efforts, organized under charitable trusts; it also involved the public sector, which he oversaw as leader of the government, promoting investment in commercial and light industrial enterprises. Indeed, this was one of the charges that the revolutionaries made against him in 1974, accusing him of abuse of power, corruption, and neglect of the population. The fact that the headway made in economic development under his watch was lost under the Dergue is a kind of poetic justice rendered to him posthumously.

## The Emperor and Education

As noted earlier, from the very beginning, the emperor saw education as a key factor in Ethiopia's development, and even its independence. He gave a considerable part of his wealth for building schools and other educational institutions, urged other wealthy people to follow his example, and encouraged students in various ways, including visiting them in their schools and asking them questions, as this writer can testify from personal experience. Until almost the end of his reign, he received in audience graduate students returning from studies abroad, quizzing them about what they studied and how they proposed to apply their knowledge for the general welfare of the people. When I returned from law studies in England, he asked me that question; I told him my wish was to practice law as a private attorney. He was not amused, and after an exchange that some who were present during the audience considered impolitic on my part, he told me with a dangerous glint in his penetrating eyes that it was payback time: I must serve in the Ministry of Justice, and that was that.

During his 1954 world tour, the emperor instructed the Ethiopian ambassador in London to arrange for a banquet in the emperor's honor. Every Ethiopian studying in Britain, including myself, was invited to the special occasion. After the banquet was over, His Majesty met every student and quizzed each on his or her area of study. After that, he spoke to the gathering in a fatherly fashion, abandoning the imperial plural and using the singular pronoun, which was rare. He called us his children that he had conceived and delivered in education ("Ba'tmhrt yeweldekuachuh lijochie"). Some of us were moved to tears.

Four years prior to that, he had inaugurated the first university college in the country—the Haile Selassie I

College, later promoted to a university and, after the emperor's fall, renamed Addis Ababa University. In quick succession, colleges of agriculture and health were opened, followed over the years by different institutions of higher education that catered to the industrial and managerial needs of the country and accompanied by the development of industrial and commercial enterprises, all of which would contribute to political and social change, including the 1974 revolution.

10

# Diplomacy

## *The American Connection and Nonalignment*

After having become a world-renowned leader with his appearance at the League of Nations in 1936, and following his return to his country and restoration to his throne after the Italian occupation, Emperor Haile Selassie made the acquisition of Eritrea (or, as some would prefer to say, its recovery) his number one diplomatic agenda. That agenda was expressed both in terms of the legitimate historical ties between Ethiopia and Eritrea and in economic and strategic terms. The economic rationale was that a landlocked Ethiopia was disadvantaged, despite the connection to the sea through the Addis Ababa–Djibouti railway, because its central and northern regions were too far from the line. Without its own outlet to the sea, the country remained a hostage to foreign powers. And in terms of the strategic imperative, recent history showed that the Eritrean region had been used repeatedly as a launching pad by foreign invaders, the latest example being Mussolini's 1935 invasion.

The pertinent questions involved in the dispute between Eritrea and Ethiopia have been rehearsed in numerous back-and-forth arguments between the two sides, played out in their bitterest form in recent times during the so-called border war of 1998–2000. At this point, it is sufficient to say that just as Emperor Haile Selassie's imperial appetite overreached itself in 1962 when he abolished the UN-arranged Ethiopia-Eritrea federation, Eritrea's current president, Isaias Afwerki, also overreached in provoking the recent war. It is ironic that in annexing Eritrea the emperor flouted the very international law and morality to which he had appealed when his own country was invaded. The Eritrean war of independence (or of secession, according to some) began following the annexation, and would haunt Emperor Haile Selassie to his last days, as it has haunted his successors. As to why Haile Selassie made the "recovery" of Eritrea his number one diplomatic agenda, one theory is that in addition to the above mentioned reasons, he was dedicated to what may be called one-upmanship—doing something that would place him in the history books above Menelik, who "sold" Eritrea to the Italians.[1] Whether this is true or not, the emperor's obsession with Eritrea did finally help cause his downfall.

**The American Connection**

The emperor first met U.S. president Franklin Roosevelt in 1945 when the latter was passing through Cairo en route back home from the Yalta meeting with Stalin and Churchill. The emperor had settled his differences with his British allies and was on friendly terms with them, but on the urging of his minister of the pen, Woldegiorgis, who distrusted the British, he flew to a meeting with Roosevelt on a warship off Suez, where he recited the problems Ethiopia was facing as well as his earnest desire that Eritrea be joined with Ethiopia. Roosevelt invited him to visit after the war and in the meantime promised to send an economic mission, which he did. This was followed by a loan and the replacement of British advisors by Americans. It was the beginning of the American connection that would dominate Ethiopia diplomacy for three decades. Roosevelt died soon thereafter, and it was during the Eisenhower presidency that Haile Selassie visited the United States, in 1954.

Perhaps the most important achievement of the emperor through American help was the decision by the United Nations to pass Resolution 390 A(V) of 1950, which joined Eritrea with Ethiopia in a lopsided federation "under the sovereignty of the Ethiopian Crown." It was that federation, brought about through the use of an international instrument, that Emperor Haile Selassie abolished in 1962, thus provoking a long and bloody war of liberation. The UN General Assembly was under an obligation to protest and insist on the reversal of the emperor's act of annexation, but failed to do so, just as the League of Nations had failed to come to Ethiopia's help when Italy committed an act of aggression in 1935. It is interesting to speculate whether Haile Selassie learned a lesson from his tragic experience of relying on international law—that it is force that matters, not law or morality. The Eritreans in turn learned the same lesson, for having unsuccessfully relied on diplomacy, they were forced to take up arms to secure their right to self-determination, which they finally achieved after thirty years of heavy sacrifice.

### Haile Selassie and Nonalignment

The nonalignment movement grew out of the response of some countries, including some newly liberated Third World nations, to the post–World War rivalry between the Soviet Union and the Western countries, led by the United States. The period known as the Cold War began in 1945 and lasted until the fall of the Soviet Union in 1989. It saw the liberation of much of Africa from European colonial rule, and soon Africa became an ideological battleground for the opposing forces. The guiding principles of the nonalignment movement were first discussed and framed at an international conference held in Bandung, Indonesia, attended by leaders such as India's Pandit Nehru, Yugoslavia's Josip Broz Tito, Egypt's Gamal Abdel Nasser, China's Chou En Lai, and Ethiopia's Haile Selassie.

### Haile Selassie and Africa

Haile Selassie was an elder statesman who had become an internationally renowned figure long before any the other African leaders who shared the platform with him in May 1963 at the creation of the Organization of African Unity (OAU). Most of the men who became leaders of their respective countries in the late 1950s and early 1960s were students when the emperor made his famous appeal to the League of Nations in Geneva in 1936. One was Nelson Mandela, who was a boy of seventeen when Mussolini conquered Ethiopia. In his memoirs, *Long Walk to Freedom*, he writes, "Ethiopia has always held a special place in my own imagination." In 1962, on the eve of the OAU summit, almost thirty years later, he was finally able to meet Haile Selassie, which, he says, was "like shaking hands with history."

Haile Selassie's failure to stop the march of fascism had made him a martyr among the peoples of the world, and in particular among Africans both in the continent and throughout the Diaspora. It also helped reinforce the emerging spirit of Pan-Africanism. Indeed, Haile Selassie's position as a martyr gave him elevated status as a leader in African affairs, particularly in the early days of decolonization, before people like Nkrumah and Nyerere began asserting themselves as leaders in the African liberation agenda. Although African liberation and unity was a universally held value in Africa, different people had different ways of achieving it. Some, feeling that the countries could not all unite across the vast continent against their colonial oppressors, preferred to fight colonialism country by country. While leaders such as Nkrumah saw unification as a goal unto itself, Haile Selassie, a late bloomer in African affairs, had to be coaxed and challenged to take up the cause of Pan-Africanism. But when he did, persuaded by his advisors, it was in earnest and with characteristic single-mindedness. When Nkrumah convened the conference of African Heads of State and Government in the spring of 1958, the emperor sent his youngest son, Prince Sahle Selassie.

Haile Selassie's engagement with Africa prompted him to establish a scholarship fund for students to study at the University College of Addis Ababa. Two hundred scholarships were awarded, and students came from West, East, and Central Africa; I taught some of them in my classes at the college. A number of these students ended up occupying important ministerial and other positions in their own countries, such as Robert Ouko of Kenya, who was foreign minister of his country until he was brutally murdered, allegedly by agents of President Daniel Arap Moi.

The emperor's government also invited leaders of African liberation movements, encouraging them and providing assistance. Young African political and labor union leaders began frequenting the Ethiopian capital, and the Ethiopian media began putting a positive spin on African liberation movements. Among the emerging leaders with whom I struck up a friendship at the time were the late Tom Mboya of Kenya and Felix Moumie of Cameroon. They all met with the emperor with the help of those of us who had formed the ad hoc African Liberation Assistance

Committee, which the emperor's government approved. Tom Mboya ended up becoming the second most important political figure in Kenya until he was assassinated by jealous rivals. Felix Moumie was poisoned by an agent of the French Secret Service. These and other African leaders like Nyerere and Kaunda enriched the political experience of Ethiopians through speeches at public as well as at private meetings that some of my friends like Richard and Rita Pankhurst and I arranged.

The culmination of the emperor's engagement with African affairs was the establishment of the OAU in May 1963. That signal event in modern African history occurred following two years of intense negotiations among African leaders, hitherto polarized along ideological and personal axes of division. The main groups were known, respectively, as the Monrovia and Casablanca group of nations; the first was generally understood to be pro-Western, while the second, including Egypt and Ghana, was said to be socialist in orientation and critical of the West. One of the achievements of the creation of the OAU was to put to rest the division by creating a body that sought to speak with one voice on behalf of the continent.

Emperor Haile Selassie, who acted as host to the conference, played a crucial role in the negotiations to unite the divided groups. The world did not expect the conference to succeed in establishing a united African body; indeed, it was assumed that African leaders were too divided culturally and politically to agree. The writer attended the conference as a member of the drafting committee of the OAU Charter and could, therefore, gauge the temper of the meeting.[2] The foreign press in particular warned of impending disaster among feuding African leaders, especially since Nkrumah had proposed the creation of a United States of Africa, which was not favorably received by most of the other delegates. The critics would be disappointed. When Nkrumah threatened to walk out of the conference, Haile Selassie worked his African magic. He called on Guinea's President Sékou Touré and, holding Touré's hand like a father and looking him in the eye, said, "Mon fils, je vous prie. Allez amenez votre frère Nkrumah" (My son, I implore you to go and bring your brother Nkrumah). Touré did not hesitate in responding, "Oui Père. Je vais essayer" (Yes, Father. I will try), and brought Nkrumah back to the conference hall to a rousing standing ovation.

Africans felt proud of the achievement of the May 1963 conference, and Emperor Haile Selassie took much of the deserved credit.

# 11

# Turning of the Tide

## *A Shaken Emperor on the Horns of a Dilemma*

### The 1960 Attempted Coup and Its Impact

It was a sunny morning in mid-December 1960. The emperor was in Brazil for a weeklong official visit. That day, the people of Ethiopia woke up to martial music on the radio at the hour when normal music should have been heard. We waited . . . and waited . . . and waited. Neighbors came to report that they saw groups of troops in battle gear being taken in jeeps toward the city center. Meanwhile, the martial music continued.

Suddenly, a radio announcer told a puzzled population to await an important announcement. I and my family and a group of friends who came to my house then heard the tired voice of the emperor's son and heir to the Solomonic throne, Crown Prince Asfa-Wosen.

Everyone in the room was shocked as the crown prince denounced the regime presided over by his royal father, a regime that he had been patiently waiting to inherit. The speech, which later turned out to have been written by Germame Neway, the Columbia University–educated intellectual and brain behind the coup attempt, was an indictment of the "oppressive feudal system," and promised to inaugurate a better system under which the crown prince would be a salaried constitutional monarch. Germame was the younger brother of General Mengistu Neway, head of the emperor's bodyguard. In addition to the Neways, the plotters included Workneh Gebeyhu, head of the emperor's intelligence service. They had arrested almost all the cabinet ministers and other dignitaries close to the imperial throne, and kept them in the palace. Germame had also summoned people whom he considered sympathetic to the revolution or fellow travelers. I later found out that my name was on the list of those who would be appointed as cabinet members following the overthrow of the emperor.[1]

The December revolt, as it became known, was the first direct challenge Haile Selassie had faced in his thirty years of rule. The fact that the revolt came from his trusted bodyguard added a painful element. More painful and a shock to the emperor was the involvement of his trusted Workneh, whom he loved like a son. The crown prince's speech, which was greeted by almost everyone with confusion and suspicion, did not seem to surprise his father, who forgave him instantly when the prince lay prostrate at his father's feet asking for forgiveness. The emperor knew that his son was being used as a puppet and had neither the courage nor the moral fiber to be martyred rather than betray his father. So he forgave him with a wry smile on his lips.

The diehard supporters of the imperial system, who had a strong vested interest in it, as well as the absentee landowners and the emperor's kinsmen, were outraged by the crown prince's action. On the other hand, my generation of Ethiopians, as well as a few disgruntled older people, welcomed the coup as a wakeup call. Some were naturally anxious about what would happen to their civil rights under a new government, considering the bad record of military regimes in human rights and the rule of law. But the general view was that nothing could be worse than what we had and that a military regime of the Nasser variety, guided by progressive individuals like Germame, would clear the way for a better republic. For those who held that view, the disappointment to come would be a bitter education. Certainly, on one point the outcome of the failed coup proved a step forward toward progress: it loosened the bonds that held the feudal system together.

The coup failed because the bulk of the armed forces and the air force remained loyal to the emperor and defeated his rebellious bodyguards. When they knew they had lost, the Neway brothers decided to take the top members of the imperial regime with them, and there was a horrendous massacre of ministers and other dignitaries in the emperor's palace in Sidist Kilo. They did not even spare Italian war hero Ras Abebe Aregai. It was later reported that when Abebe Aregai challenged Germame's right to treat him the way he did, denying him water to drink, for instance, Germame brought him water and then reminded Ras Abebe of the guerrilla fighters who had made him a hero and whom he had forgotten. The exact words related to me by a survivor were "Did you think of the peasants who sold their oxen and followed you and who made you Ras?"

The principal coup makers were either killed or captured a few days after the rebellion had failed. Germame was killed resisting arrest some fifty miles south of Addis Ababa. Workneh committed suicide, and General Mengistu was wounded and captured. His trial became the object of great curiosity and a bellwether of what would happen to the other rebel officers. Most of them, as it turned out, were banished and put under detention in distant places for several years.

### The Loosening of the Bonds

Despite its failure, the coup had an impact on government and society, as well as implications for future changes. Its impact on government was felt first in the shape and behavior of the executive. The massacre of most of the cabinet members left the government truncated; the whole government system was shaken, and the bureaucracy was left dithering for some time. The emperor decided to donate his palace, the scene of a bloody massacre, to the university. Perhaps a more profound effect of the coup was that it released the suppressed energy of the public and emboldened progressive voices. One manifestation of this was student activities, which were the most threatening to the imperial regime. Students began organizing poetry festivals in which the content of the poems was revolutionary, lamenting the condition of the oppressed peasants. In these poems and in other forms of popular expression, Germame and his associates acquired the status of martyrs.

The military and the labor unions, too, were aroused. With the assistance of university students and teachers, labor unions began organizing clandestinely and demanding better wages and conditions of work, threatening strikes. True to his ability to adapt to new situations, the emperor decided to appear as an advocate of full union rights, and ordered his prime minister to prepare what became the Labor Relations Proclamation of 1963, which, while giving labor unions hitherto unknown rights, created mechanisms of control for the government. Still, the law represented progress; previously, companies could hire and fire with no legal redress, leading to periodic confrontations and violence, but the law now provided for mutual accommodation between unions on the one hand and employers and the government on the other.

The December 1960 coup created a whole host of challenges, of which the most important was the issue of security. For the first year after the coup, the emperor and his principal advisors were principally concerned with survival. After all, it was his most trusted aides who had revolted against him. He was particularly stung by Workneh's involvement. For a long time he was in denial, often remarking that Workneh must have been compelled to go along with Germame's scheme under duress. He had been especially fond of Workneh, part of whose duties, in fact, had been to spy on the top military brass, including General Mengistu of the bodyguards. The emperor's survival strategy included distrust of even his closest kinsmen, on the basis of the Machiavellian dictum "If I take care of my close friends, I can take care of my enemies." (The emperor was an avid reader of Machiavelli; Workneh told this writer that the emperor lent him an Amharic translation of *The Prince.*)

A matter of great significance after the coup situation was the disposal of hundreds of officers and enlisted men and some civilians who had taken part in it. This raised security issues as well as legal questions related to land reform, administration of justice, and constitutional reform. A military general was appointed on a temporary basis to deal with the security issues. The decimation of the cabinet and the dissolution of the imperial bodyguard had left a vacuum in the government system, which was filled by ambitious and willful men like Ras Asrate Kassa, son of the emperor's loyal kinsman Ras Kassa. Asrate was openly disdainful as well as resentful of the "commoners" whom the emperor had raised to positions of prominence, such as the prime minister and other ministers. In the twilight period during the year following the coup, in which the emperor temporarily lost his bearings and became vulnerable, Asrate had himself appointed head of a commission dealing with the disposal of all cases related to the rebellion, and in particular focusing on the rebellious officers.

## Impact of the December Coup on the Imperial System

Apart from the decimation of the government's top personnel, what impact did the coup have on the system? All progressively inclined people had great expectations, believing that the emperor, shaken by what had happened, would allow political and social changes. The wily emperor raised their hopes by throwing a few crumbs, so to speak. He ordered the creation of several commissions tasked with bringing about changes, such as a Commission on Land Reform, a Commission on Judicial Reform, and a Commission on Social Reform. The commissions started their work promisingly for three to four months, then gradually ceased their operations with no explanation provided. The Commission on Land Reform created the expectation for many people, including the writer, who was a member of the Commission on Judicial Reform, that the peasants might finally be given land rights. But it all came to naught; despite his proclaimed intentions, His Majesty was not willing or able to alienate the class that was the backbone of the imperial system. For many of us, it was a moment of truth that showed the emperor's true colors, dashing our hopes for real social change.

As for political change, things continued for some five years before the emperor introduced cosmetic changes in the cabinet system. The prime minister was given the power to nominate his ministers for appointment by the emperor; previously, the emperor chose the ministers, and the prime ministers had no role in the process. Writing a commentary, in a British legal journal, this writer voiced his disappointment, and paid for it by being banished to a distant province for three years.

Most people settled down to live with the status quo, except for the university student activists, joined by high school students, who continued demands for change. "Meriet l'arashu" (land to the tiller) was their mantra. Their protests kept gathering strength until they were joined by the military, which had its own complaints, including insufficient salaries that did not meet the challenges of runaway inflation and the fact that their love for their commander-in-chief seem to be unrequited. Everything seemed to point to revolution, and everyone expressed fear of an impending disaster: everyone, that is, except the eighty-two-year-old emperor.

### On the Horns of a Dilemma

For anyone who had followed the ups and downs of Emperor Haile Selassie's career and seen the dogged but supple manner in which he responded to different challenges to his position and even to his life, his response to the attempted coup of December 1960 was disappointing.

He had set the clock for real changes that might have left a brilliant legacy to mark his famed life and career. The Rases had been tamed, whatever residue of power was left to them by the 1931 constitution having been finished off by five years of Italian occupation. And after the restoration, he passed legislation that introduced administrative structures and organizations that opened the way for real changes. He proclaimed the 1955 Revised Constitution, which provided the framework for the changes that he had spoken about throughout his career. Then, when the moment of truth arrived—the hour of real decision—he retreated to a comfort zone, siding with the traditional forces that he had fought for decades.

Why did he retreat? To answer this, we must ask why, not just how, he achieved and maintained his power, including the reason why he stood in opposition to the conservative forces in the first place. As to how, it is instructive to cite the seventeenth-century English poet Andrew Marvell. In his "Horatian Ode upon Cromwell's Return from Ireland" (quoted above as an epigraph to chapter 4), he wrote, "The same arts that did gain / A power, must it maintain." The political skills of Tafari / Haile Selassie exemplify and confirm Marvell's poetic insight.

## Between Progress and Absolute Power

From the time he sought and ascended to the Ethiopian throne, Haile Selassie (then called Tafari) appeared to the world as a progressive prince dedicated to bringing his country into the modern world. All observers agree on his success in taming the traditional nobility by imposing upon them modern ideas and institutions, and in creating a centralized administration that curtailed their power, if not eliminated it. Throughout most of his reign he was generally considered a progressive statesman; and the status of martyr he gained in consequence of the Italian invasion added a peculiar mystique to his power. That mystique and his progressive reputation sheltered him from the critical appraisal that all statesmen receive, but the 1960 attempted coup and his response opened him up for serious criticism even from people considered friendly to him and his government.

Within Ethiopia, radical student movements demanding "land to the tiller" raised questions about the emperor's power and his attitude toward the continued power of the traditional forces who abused the impoverished peasants. If he is a progressive leader, they asked, why does he allow such abuse, and when would he cause changes to be made so that peasants had rights in land tenure? By the time of the 1960 attempted coup, such questions had become part of the daily discourse among the literati, and after the coup failed, the students' repeated demands for change on the land question became the emperor's nightmare. Those demands reverberated throughout the empire, and the labor unions and the armed forces began to voice sympathy and gradual support for them. It is an irony of history that these, the very products of his modernization programs, became his most persistent critics, and would eventually combine to end his rule, as we shall see in the next chapter. It was a sign of the emperor's loss of control and of a weakening of his critical faculties that he did not give these demands the attention they deserved. Close observers of the imperial palace scene suggested that by the late 1960s the emperor had lost his phenomenal memory, with some even saying that he was affected by some form of dementia.

Another issue in daily conversation was the inordinate amount of time and energy the emperor was spending in travel, mostly to other African countries. His success in helping establish the Organization of African Unity (OAU) and his mediation in the Algeria-Morocco territorial dispute had established him as an elder statesman and whetted his appetite to engage in African affairs more frequently. In their petitions to the emperor, some Ethiopians started referring to him as Africa's Father. But critics complained that, like a wayward husband, he was neglecting his first duty to his spouse, Ethiopia, in favor of his mistress, Africa. People close to the palace claimed that he was annoyed by the constant attacks leveled at him by student radicals and other critics, considering them ungrateful ruffians who did not know what they were talking about. And the palace sycophants continually massaged his ego, while his ministers would not confront him with the reality. Those who did ended up being dismissed or "frozen." He had also become unresponsive to reasonable proposals that he had accepted gracefully in the past. In other words, he had become more autocratic. As Bahru Zewde, a distinguished Ethiopian historian, has put it, "the progressive and reactionary features of [Haile Selassie]'s reign are not mutually exclusive but tend to overlap. Power, which remained the abiding concern of the emperor, was their locus of interaction. In the long run, his obsession with power lent reactionary character to what at the outset could have been regarded as progressive measures." Bahru adds that the political centralization, once considered to be an instrument of progress in the Ethiopian setting, "negated the legitimate wishes of regions and nationalities for internal autonomy."[2]

# 12

# Last Days

## *Revolution and the End of the Monarchy*

### The Gathering Storm

For over a decade before the revolution in early spring 1974, the country was beset by student agitation and labor union demands for fair labor practices and improvements in working conditions. There were also regional rebellions, with the war in Eritrea posing the most serious threat to imperial rule. Then, more ominously, there began to be grumblings in the armed forces, quiet at first, but growing louder. In these protests, the name of the emperor was invoked at first with respect, in the expectation that he would settle the grievances. The emperor was still seen as the dispenser of justice and equity, and his minions as selfish rascals who were betraying his trust. But the emperor's failure to respond finally led to more radical demands.

### Student Movement

The first to question the emperor's legitimacy and boldly and unambiguously declare the imperial system to be the source of all the country's problems were the university students. By the mid-1960s, student organizations within Ethiopia as well as in America and Europe were espousing Marxist ideology, demanding social and political change. Within the student movement, divisions emerged based on disagreements on objectives and tactics. Some favored an evolutionary model, with social democracy as the objective and peaceful democratic change as the method. Others, who ultimately commanded the majority voice, insisted on radical reconstruction through Marxist strategy and tactics. Lenin's famous tract *What Is to Be Done?* was first in the list of works examined by student study groups and adopted as the means of achieving the aims of the revolution. Marxism-Leninism, the gospel of twentieth-century leftist revolutionaries, became the standard, which necessarily meant the rejection of "bourgeois" democratic aims and methods.

Inevitably, a split occurred in the movement, later complicated by the split between Soviet Union and China. The emperor's intelligence service, by that time expertly advised by American and Israeli professionals, saw in it an opportunity to weaken the student movement and thus postpone, if not prevent, the eventual revolution. The split arose from a disagreement between the faction whose leaders lived in the United States and the faction whose leaders lived in Europe. Attempting to find a real difference between the pronouncements of the two groups, each grounded in leftist scripture, is like reading the different pronouncements of Roman Catholic and Eastern Orthodox Christians at the time of the historic schism. To neutral observers, it was a case of a difference without a distinction. As with the split of Russian revolutionaries into Bolshevik and Menshevik factions, the difference was over tactics, including the issue of membership. A hidden struggle for power developed; it was as if Russian history were repeating itself in Ethiopia.

The two factions became known as the Ethiopian People's Revolutionary Party (EPRP), whose leaders were based in America, and the All-Ethiopia Socialist Movement (Meison, an acronym for the group's name in Amharic), whose leaders were based in Europe. The EPRP commanded the majority of supporters within the country, and the relative strength of the two factions would determine their respective behavior when the revolution exploded in 1974, as we shall see. Each faction published pamphlets in attempts to recruit followers, particularly within the country. The EPRP's popular pamphlet, called *Democracia*, was published in Amharic; its editors were outstanding writers, including poets, in the Amharic language. Meison published a pamphlet called *Sefiew Hisb* (Broad masses), which was not as widely distributed. Both factions endeavored to recruit followers within and outside government circles, which gave the imperial intelligence service a means to monitor and exploit the differences between them.

In the final phase of the revolutionary adventure, the larger and more popular EPRP would decide to adopt the Maoist strategy of conducting a rural guerrilla insurgency, working with the peasants and gradually encircling the state and capturing power. In the final phase of that strategy, the EPRP itself would split into two factions, one keeping to the Maoist strategy and the other wishing to conduct urban guerrilla warfare and overthrow the military government that had taken over from the emperor. Meison, in turn, decided to collaborate with the military government, which further complicated the role of the student movement and ultimately resulted in mutually inflicted damage, to the delight of the government.

### The Emperor's Interest

The final fate of both factions is part of the tragic story of the misadventure of the student movement, which had started with much fanfare and great expectations for a transition to a democratic postimperial system. Throughout the events, the emperor continued to practice his well-honed skills of divide and rule, even as his reactions were being slowed, his knowledge of the facts was incomplete, and his analytical powers were diminished by advancing age. In July 1969, the present writer was summoned by the emperor to his palace in Dire Dawa, during his annual retreat, to be harangued about the fallacy of the student demands for socialism. His government, he said, had put in place national institutions like the Imperial Highway Authority, the National Airlines, and the Imperial Board of Telecommunications. Was that not socialism? What else did the students want? To my response that I did not know, he vehemently asserted that I did indeed know but was being cagy. (What he actually said, in Amharic, was "Debaqqi, shemmaqi," which is quite a bit more strident than "cagy.") I stood silent; there was nothing I could say, given the tone of his remarks. When he pressed me for an answer, I replied that the institutions he mentioned did indeed contain aspects of socialism. It was an answer given under duress, but I knew there was an element of truth in it, for a classic definition of socialism is public ownership of the means of production, distribution, and exchange. What I did not, could not, say was that the critical question was who the beneficiary of these institutions was! Before he dismissed me, the emperor seemed to relent, and asked me about my work as mayor of Harar.

That His Imperial Majesty would summon someone whom he had banished to a province far from the center was a sign of how desperate he was feeling. I couldn't help being sorry for this man, who at the ripe old age of seventy-seven felt cornered by the aggressive demands for change voiced by students and labor unions, beset by social forces that were the products of his own modernizing programs. In some of their demands, the students used language that could hardly be described as polite or respectful to the man whom much of the world respected and the majority of his subjects seemed to adore. The constitution stated that his dignity was inviolable, but clearly the student radicals did not care about that. What a comedown!

From his perspective, bitterness and a feeling of betrayal were understandable; but not from the perspective of those who saw his autocracy as an obstacle to progress. That difference in perspective was created not only by ideological disagreements, but also by a generational change with regard to how one ought to address an emperor who also happened to be an elder and therefore deserving respect in accordance with traditional values.

To what extent their Marxist-Leninist ideology, with class struggle as the critical imperative, influenced the students' lack of respect is anybody's guess.

## Labor Unions

Just as the students were a product of the emperor's education programs, of which he was rightfully proud, the labor unions were the products of his programs for building the industrial, manufacturing, and commercial enterprises that largely came into being during his reign, if not completely at his behest. He may not have consciously wished for the emergence of the social forces that eventually would lead to demands for change; but his modernizing programs gave rise to them, and he thus had some legitimate right to claim that he was ultimately responsible for their creation.

Was he also responsible for responding to the workers' claims for fair and equitable treatment from their employers? There's the rub; the emperor's private interests, suitably camouflaged by his charitable organization, the Haile Selassie Charitable Trust, as well as the interests of members of the royal family and their hangers-on, inevitably clashed with the interests of the workers, despite the claims made by his agents that the workers were being treated neutrally and equitably even where their interests were opposed to his. Again, the writer was a witness to the invisible hands that brought pressure to bear in favor of the interests of the emperor and of those associated with the imperial system. In 1968, I was an umpire in a labor dispute between the Ethiopian factory workers of the Japanese-managed cotton factory in Dire Dawa and the company's management. The governor of the region warned me that I should decline the appointment as umpire. I did not decline, and as a result was subjected to all kinds of subtle and not-so-subtle pressures to deliver a verdict that favored the company. I resisted those pressures and handed down a verdict that satisfied the legitimate claim of the factory workers, which the Japanese management found to be fair and acceptable. I gambled in relying on the rhetorical commitment of His Majesty to the rule of law and due process—and I won. Far from being punished, I was told indirectly (by the governor—my "jailer"—who had been against my involvement in the arbitration) that in that arbitration dispute justice was rendered and the major shareholder, the emperor's charitable organization, was satisfied with the award.

The emperor's attitude toward the emergence of organized labor was pragmatic; as was his habit, he accepted the inevitable unless it posed a real threat to his power. After many years of hesitation, he was finally persuaded that it was time to legally recognize the labor unions. By doing so, and creating a mechanism of mediation to settle disputes, it might be possible for government and employers to control the unions more effectively. And so it was; the creation of a nationwide labor organization, the Center of Ethiopian Labor Unions (CELU), resulted in a period of peaceful coexistence of management and labor for a number of years, until the leadup to the revolution in 1974, when the CELU joined the chorus of demands for political change.

## Regional Rebellions

Rebellions occurred in regions across the country, mostly caused by maladministration or mistreatment by local authorities of influential elites, or inspired by irredentist sentiments, as in the Harar and Bale regions. But, as mentioned above, by far the most serious rebellion was in Eritrea, later joined by that in the neighboring Tigray region. What made it more serious was that what the Eritreans demanded was complete independence from Ethiopia, as well as the military strength of the fighters there, the support they received from the people, and the region's geographical location along the Red Sea. The powerful Eritrean People's Liberation Front (EPLF) would join with the Tigray People's Liberation Front (TPLF), the next most strongly armed political organization in the area, which would become the major organization to form a coalition government after the fall of the military government in 1991.

Eritrea was an Italian colony until its liberation by the Allied forces in 1941. As noted in a previous chapter, the Eritreans were the victims of a U.S.-instigated scheme that had the effect of denying their legitimate claim to independence when they were joined with Ethiopia under a UN-arranged federal structure in which Emperor Haile Selassie's government had the upper hand. Even the modicum of autonomy given under the UN-sponsored scheme was taken away when the emperor unilaterally abolished the federation, declaring Eritrea a mere province. The result was a war that lasted thirty years.

The emperor's action prompted an Eritrean sage and respected elder by the name of Asmach Mirach to make a memorable comment: "How foolish the Shoans [Ethiopians] are! They have swallowed a piece of hard rock that will destroy them." In the war's last phase, on the eve of a decisive battle, a commander of the Eritrean regiment was ordered by the high command to attack the formidable Ethiopian regiment known as Nadow. The following morning, he told his soldiers that the day of battle would be the funeral of Nadow. Such was the sense of pride and determination of Eritreans with respect to their rights—such their clarity and passion.

Emperor Haile Selassie and his government were dead certain that Ethiopia would win the war. His army, next to that of Egypt, was the strongest in Africa, and almost every observer concluded that the guerrilla army of the small nation of Eritrea was doomed to failure. In battle after battle, the emperor's forces sent waves of attacks, killing people and animals and even poisoning wells. A quarter of the population fled to neighboring countries as refugees. But instead of submitting, the Eritrean fighters and the people behind them only grew stronger, drawing the invading forces further and further into a harsh landscape. By the eve of the Ethiopian revolution, an exhausted and dispirited Ethiopian army was caught in a murderous battle in Sahel, the base area of the guerrillas, where it suffered huge losses of dead and wounded.

That was the spring of 1973, the year when the Horn of Africa, including Eritrea and Ethiopia, was hit by a two-year drought that devastated the land and left the population desperately in need of food. The emperor's government was not able or willing to supply the necessary food, and an estimated one million Ethiopians in the northern regions of Wollo and Tigray died in the famine. The fickle international press was suddenly galvanized by the sight of emaciated bodies, and reported the plight of the people to a general public outcry the world over. Notably, a British TV and radio journalist named Jonathan Dimbleby made a film that caused an uproar in Europe and America. Confronted with the question why the government did nothing to prevent the deaths of so many Ethiopians, the minister of information denied that there was famine.

## The Revolt of the Armed Forces

At the same time, word of the disaster in Sahel had reached not only the Ministry of Defense but all units of the armed forces, and it set in motion a serious rebellion in the military. "Sympathy strikes" occurred instantly, in which soldiers voiced complaints about their own conditions of service, which were deplorable. In the Negalle Borena region, the noncommissioned officers (NCOs) and enlisted men took the unprecedented step of detaining their superior officers and asking the government to send an inspecting team. The government sent the chief of staff of the armed forces, and the rebellious soldiers detained him as well. The news of the Negalle soldiers' action spread, and set off a chain reaction; the forces in Eritrea also detained their commanding officers, and others followed suit. The high command and the government felt helpless to do anything.

The next stage was critical in the unfolding of the revolution of 1974. All the units of the armed forces began to communicate with one another, breaking a pattern of discipline and the chain of command. They then agreed to choose representatives to send to the capital to guide the progress of the revolution.

The original demands of the rebelling military were couched in the trade union mode of demands for the improvement of working conditions—higher salaries, affordable housing, family allowances, medical services, and so on. But members of civil society, including students and teachers, began to call on the military to push their demands beyond their own narrow interests. The crescendo of protests continued to build. The students became more daring, and were rewarded by open public support, including that of labor unions and small traders. Coincidentally, inflation had struck at every sector of urban society, following a worldwide rise in oil prices. All were now geared for change. And as a result of the war in Eritrea and the famine in Wollo and Tigray, Ethiopia had become the center of world attention.

By late 1973, Addis Ababa's nervous system was showing signs of breakdown and paranoia. People hoarded essential supplies. Absenteeism from school and work, disobedience of authority, bold exchanges of obscenities, the flight of capital, and the purchase of goods at astronomical prices became the order of the day. Other large cities soon followed suit.

## The Quickening March of Events

As 1973 gave way to 1974, the pace of the revolution was accelerating. A brief chronology of events in early 1974 will give a picture of the irreversible slide of the imperial regime toward its demise.

*Thursday, February 21*

Tension was mounting. Government employees failed to report to work due to a lack of transportation. There were reports of random shootings. Two students were killed by soldiers guarding buses and installations, and soldiers toting machine guns on open army trucks patrolled the streets. The government announced on radio and television the suspension of the World Bank–initiated Education Sector Review, which had aroused public opposition, led by the teachers unions, who argued that it would put nine- and ten-year-old children (of the poor) to work after only four years of education.

*Friday, February 22*

More soldiers were visible everywhere. The prime minister's car was stoned, along with those of other dignitaries. Shops were closed. Buses were back in service, escorted by armed guards. Fear crippled the city—the fear of the unknown.

*Saturday, February 23*

The emperor appeared on TV and radio, announcing the suspension of the new education policy and a reduction in oil prices.

*Sunday, February 24*

The streets were deserted. The government had arrested one thousand taxi drivers who had demonstrated protesting high gas prices. The soldiers, now everywhere, were coordinating, not opposing, the stone-throwing students. More cars were smashed. On the evening news it was announced that the salary of soldiers would be raised to $100 a month (then equivalent to US$20), comparable with salaries of other civil service employees, effective in March.

*Monday, February 25*

There was a mass promotion of officers, and some of the officers were taken to the palace to thank the emperor.

*Tuesday, February 26*

Early in the morning, it was reported that the ground forces in Asmara, the Eritrean capital, had mutinied. The soldiers, having seen that the emperor had no clothes, demanded a monthly salary of $150. Some also demanded political changes and dismissal of ministers and generals. The Asmara soldiers arrested all officers above the rank of captain.

*Wednesday, February 27*

The air force and navy officers joined in the mutiny, and a delegation was dispatched from Addis Ababa to negotiate terms and conditions of release of the officers. Only one member of the delegation returned; the rest were detained. On television it was announced that the government of Prime Minister Aklilu had asked to resign and that the emperor was considering the request.

*Thursday, February 28*

Troops were sent to guard important installations, including the Ministry of Information, the banks, and the airport. At two p.m., the emperor read a short speech announcing the appointment of a new prime minister. This was followed by an announcement of more salary increases.

As the above blow-by-blow recitation of developments shows, things were falling apart; the center no longer held. Soldiers were now everywhere, stopping cars and checking identity papers.

An OAU meeting of African foreign ministers was postponed because the government could not guarantee their safety.

Endalkachew Makonnen, the new prime minister, an Oxford-educated aristocrat, made an unsuccessful attempt to bring the situation under control. Students gathered at the Arat Kilo campus in Addis Ababa shouted demands for his removal. The students had been brought by soldiers, who urged them to keep up their demands.

On March 1, more students demonstrated, and shots were fired, with some students killed. Confusion followed. The armed forces were divided between a minority who supported the new prime minister and a majority who wanted him out.

The new prime minister appointed a new cabinet whose composition reflected an attempt to bridge the gap between the old and the new, between the emerging middle class and the retreating nobility. In this he seemed to continue the policy of the emperor, with the difference that young technocrats predominated in the cabinet. Many believed that had the emperor done this a year before, the country might have welcomed it as a great leap forward. As it was, the unleashed forces would not be satisfied with what they considered cosmetic changes. Above all, the military was now out to grasp power in its own name.

On March 1, the emperor addressed the nation, promising constitutional reform. But his promises were drowned out in the clamor for radical change. The same day, the labor unions staged a countrywide general strike. Even clergymen struck for pay raises.

## Emergence of the Dergue

As the situation went from bad to worse, people started talking about a shadowy coordinating committee of the military that was directing events and controlling or influencing the forces of change. The members of this committee, later known as the Dergue (Amharic for "committee"), numbered 120 and came from the rank and file, the NCOs, and the junior officers, up to the rank of captain, of the entire military: the army, the police, and even the militia, traditionally looked down upon by the military establishment. With no organized political parties to challenge them, it was as if the revolution landed in their lap.

As membership expanded beyond the original leaders who had initiated the revolt, rivalry and competition for leadership caused the core body to reaffirm its power and elect as chairman an individual the leaders saw as lacking a strong social base and therefore malleable. It proved to be a tragic mistake. It was thus that in June 1974, an obscure man with the rank of captain, who had a reputation for drunken brawling, emerged as the leader of the Dergue. His name was Mengistu Hailemariam. Mengistu and his enthusiastic supporters made certain that all power was tightly controlled by his inner circle. Even the popular General Aman Andom, who had acted as the gray eminence advising the Dergue on strategy and tactics, was to be kept out. Not only had he outlived his usefulness, but he stood in the way of Mengistu, who turned out to be what no one had anticipated: an ambitious man determined to ascend to the summit of power.

Mengistu, no doubt aware of Aman's popularity, consented to his being named acting head of state and minister of defense following the fall of Endalkachew's new government. Endalkachew and his predecessor's cabinet ministers were arrested, together with many prominent civilians and high-ranking military officers. Nor did the Dergue allow Aman to stay in his position long. On September 12, 1974, six months after the revolution broke out, the Dergue announced the overthrow of the emperor's regime and its replacement by a constitutional monarchy. As a sop to fans of constitutional democracy, in what one historian has called a cruel joke, the emperor's ailing son, Crown Prince Asfa-Wosen, was named monarch.[1]

## The End

So what some commentators called the "creeping coup" came to an end. Emperor Haile Selassie was pushed off the stage of history, which he had dominated for over half a century. All hopes of establishing a civilian democratic system after the end of his rule were dashed when the Dergue established a military government. They called it a provisional military administration, but few were under any illusions that the military would give up power. As twenty years of African history have shown, once they have tasted power, the military rarely give it up. And those civilian political forces that might have answered hopes of civilian-based democracy were engaged in mutual recriminations that later degenerated into a murderous factional war, encouraged by the Dergue. But that is another story.

In the preface, I described the scene when the emperor was overthrown by the Dergue. On that sunny September day in 1974, the military of Ethiopia, who had sworn oaths of loyalty to their emperor and commander-in-chief, consigned a man of history to the dustbin and became men of history themselves. News that the emperor had been deposed had been broadcast on the radio early that morning. The city was mad with joyous celebration.

People left their work and shops and streamed to the emperor's Jubilee Palace, as if driven by an inner force to become part of history. Those among the motley crowd who had a sense of balance and decency were astounded by the extreme reaction of the public. But theirs was the small voice of conscience in the midst of a mob. The military had prepared the stage over months of hostile propaganda demystifying the emperor, including showing film of him feeding cows at a time when people were dying of famine in parts of the country. Their clever work stripped him of his clothes, to vary the metaphor, and left the emperor stark naked!

As they took him in a Volkswagen Beetle to his place of detention, the crowd shouted words of abuse. A rumor would circulate that the emperor told his captors in the car that his beloved people thought the palace was being robbed, and that was why they were shouting, "Robber! Robber! Robber!" If the rumor is true, it means he had taken leave of reality and retreated into an inner world. He remained in detention for some months before he was taken to the old palace, Menelik's Ghibbi, where he died one year after his overthrow.

The manner of his death is shrouded in mystery. There is a story that he was quietly murdered by Mengistu and secretly buried underneath the office from which Mengistu would rule Ethiopia for seventeen years, before being overthrown by the combined forces of the EPLF and EPRDF. When former servants of the emperor informed the new government about his secret burial, they had the decency to disinter his remains and allow him to be buried properly beside the tomb of his beloved Empress Menen.

However Emperor Haile Selassie died, it was a lonely death, with few to mourn him. Most of his relatives were either dead, exiled, or in detention, and his ministers and the palace hangers-on were detained or dispersed. It was reported that at the time of the reburial of his remains, there was only one blood relative openly mourning for him: his granddaughter (the illegitimate daughter of his late son Makonnen). It is also noteworthy that representatives of the Rastafarians were present on the occasion.

# Conclusion

The pathos of the emperor's lonely death must have shocked and saddened all who admired him, Ethiopians and non-Ethiopians. To those who followed his career closely, however, it is a tragic reminder of the fact that he was a lonely man in much of what he did all his life. It was an integral part of the mystique of his majesty. (It was not without reason that his title was "His Imperial Majesty.") He always made his decisions alone, never divulging his views or plans even to his closest confidants. All decisions made by the young Tafari while struggling to ascend to the throne, or by the older Haile Selassie, served one goal—gaining and maintaining power. The means he deployed to gain power, including intellectual and monetary resources, were amazing. The way he disposed of threats by some of the traditional nobility, such as Dejasmach Balcha, was masterly. And he exhibited incredible calm throughout the struggle to ascend to the throne and to guard it against adversaries. These qualities were, to a large extent, forged during his orphaned childhood, "steeled by adversity," as the title of a chapter of this book puts it.

Was Haile Selassie a progressive modernizer who shaped Ethiopia's destiny? The answer to this question is undoubtedly in the positive. Did his pursuit of power reflect a commitment to a higher purpose, such as modernization and centralization of the Ethiopian state? This too must be answered in the positive, despite some opposed views that contend that his use of power was purely for selfish ends that went against the interests of the nation. One commentator divides the record of the emperor's policies and politics into a progressive phase and a reactionary phase, concluding that his progressive phase ended in 1955 with the promulgation of the Revised Constitution. According to this view, the acquisition and maintenance of power was "a matter of obsessive concern" to the emperor. In other words, he did not stand for progress for its own sake, "but rather that progress was a concomitant of his quest for power."[1]

On this view, even the centralization of the state, which meant destroying or diminishing the power of the reactionary forces opposed to progress, was not altogether altruistic but was pursued in the service of monopolizing power, and had a negative side, denying people the exercise of regional power. The better view seems to be that such a judgment needs to take into account the historical circumstances. The emperor's unwarranted abolition of the federation of Ethiopia and Eritrea, for example, was an unfortunate example of a decision taken in pursuit of personal (imperial) power that ended tragically. The argument that the emperor's policy, beginning with the 1943 decree, which consummated Haile Selassie's early modernizing and centralizing aims, was in accordance with the needs of an underdeveloped state is justified, in my view.

The consensus is that the denial of democracy is the central issue on which the emperor finally stumbled. Democracy was one of the exciting promises of his earlier work, and in refusing to grant more power to the central institutions of the state, including the cabinet and the parliament, he certainly chose personal power over national interest. This was indeed his principal failure as a leader, and contributed to his tragic end. Perhaps a more critical cause of his fall was his inability or unwillingness to change the condition of the Ethiopian masses, who lived in abject poverty contrasted with the few who monopolized land and other resources. The rapid decline of his authority in the last days of his reign, the disrespect shown by the mob, and his ignominious end should be a lesson to actual and would-be autocrats. For what was once considered an impregnable imperial edifice crumbled like the walls of ancient Jericho at the sound of Joshua's trumpets.

*Tafari with his father, Ras Makonnen, who raised the motherless child, ca. 1905*

*The newly crowned King Tafari, 1928*

*The emperor in his exile years, appearing before the League of Nations to plead his country's case, 1936*

*Emperor Haile Selassie, mid- to late 1950s*

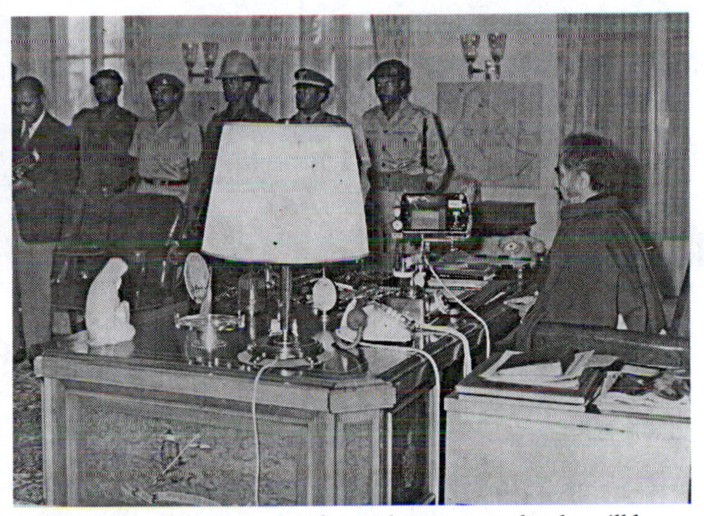

*A delegation of the Dergue informs the emperor that he will be removed from the palace, 1974 (courtesy of Tsehai Publishers)*

# Notes

## Preface

1. Bereket Habte Selassie, *The Crown and the Pen.*

2. The author, who was a close friend and confidant of General Aman Andom, was privy to information about the general's attempts, via Ras Imru, to convince the emperor to relinquish his funds in Swiss bank accounts.

3. Ras Imru's memoirs were edited by Fekade Azeze.

## Chapter 1: Leadership in the Context of Ethiopian History and Mythology

1. In an unpublished paper, Donald Levine suggests geographical distance as a source of legitimacy. A copy of the paper is in the author's possession.

2. Imru, *Kayehut, Kemastawsew.*

3. The reference is to Ato Gaitachew Bekele.

## Chapter 3: Harar, Ras Makonnen, and Menelik's Court

1. The victory of Menelik's army over that of Emir Abdullahi and the exchange of notes between the two on the eve of the battle of Chelenko are the subjects of legends. One legend is that the emir advised Menelik to convert to Islam if he wanted to receive the victorious emir's mercy

after the battle. For Menelik's response, see Monfreid, *Ménélik tel qu'il fut.*

## Chapter 4: The Feud with Iassu—the Plot Thickens

1. Thesiger, *Life of My Choice.*
2. See Selassie, *My Life and Ethiopia's Progress,* 1:44.
3. Prouty, *Empress Taytu and Menilek II,* 337.

## Chapter 5: The 1916 Coup d'État and the Rise of a Man of Destiny

1. Menelik is considered the creator of modern Ethiopia, a much expanded version of the core part of ancient Ethiopia. Many Ethiopians believe that what Menelik accomplished was not conquest but a recovery of what had been lost.
2. See Imru, *Kayehut, Kemastawsew,* 61–66.
3. Ibid., 27.
4. Ibid.
5. *Teqil* was Tafari's *yeferess sem* (nom de guerre).
6. See Selassie, *My Life and Ethiopia's Progress,* 1:83. In his visit to Aden, he was able to fly in an airplane and was also given an exhibition of bombing from the air, something that he used to good advantage a few years later in a conflict with a local feudal lord. He also used bombing against a rebellion in northern Ethiopia, for which he was criticized.
7. Mosley, *Haile Selassie,* 123, citing Rey, *In the Country of the Blue Nile.*
8. Ibid., 122.

## Chapter 6: From King to Emperor

1. Haile Selassie is his baptismal name, which is recited by priests during the funeral service. All Christians of the Orthodox denomination are given baptismal names.

2. Cited in Mosley, *Haile Selassie*. 163.

3. By tradition, "invited guests" are required to obtain the permission of the host before departing. It would amount to the crime of lèse-majesté to break this custom.

4. Cited in Mosley, *Haile Selassie*, 172.

5. Ibid.

## Chapter 7: The Italian Invasion and the Emperor's Exile

1. De Bono, *Anno XIII*, cited in Mosley, *Haile Selassie*, 176.

2. For a detailed description of the Italo-Ethiopian War of 1936, see Steer, *Caesar in Abyssinia*, cited in Mosley, *Haile Selassie*, 188–99.

3. I am indebted to my friend Mezgbu G. Amlak for bringing Campbell's book to my attention.

## Chapter 8: World War II and the Return of the Emperor to Ethiopia

1. Cited in Mosley, *Haile Selassie*, 246.

2. Ibid., 250.

3. Ibid., 251. The Amharic version of the speech is more poetic.

4. Mosley, *Haile Selassie*, 251–52.

## Chapter 9: Postliberation Developments

1. Getachew, *Beyond the Throne*.

2. Farago, *Abyssinia on the Eve*, 70–71, quoted in Makonnen Tegegn, "Walda-Giyorgis Walda-Yohannes," 135.

3. That the emperor did not take kindly to criticism of his laws is borne out by my own experiences with him. In 1966 he banished me to Harar for three years as a result of a critique I wrote in a British law journal on his "reform" of the cabinet system.

4. See my memoirs, *The Crown and the Pen*, especially chap. 10.

## Chapter 10: Diplomacy: The American Connection and Nonalignment

1. Eritrea became an Italian colony in January 1889, when the Italian government consolidated its conquest of the area, giving it the name Eritrea. The conquest began with the acquisition of the port of Asab by an Italian company, which later relinquished it to the government, and gradually expanded from the Red Sea area to the highlands, ending in the declaration establishing the colony. Throughout, there had been military engagements in which the forces of Emperor Yohannes thwarted earlier Italian attempts at conquest. But Yohannes was killed fighting the Sudanese Dervishes in 1889, and Menelik succeeded him. The claim that Menelik "sold" Eritrea is related to Menelik's dealings with the Italians, obtaining from them arms and ammunition and expanding the empire southward while Yohannes was engaged in defending the country against foreign incursions. People ask: Why didn't Menelik press his advantage to push the Italians out following his victory over them at Adwa in 1896? From this question follows the conclusion that he "sold" Eritrea to the Italians. This is one of the endlessly debated questions among Ethiopians.

2. As a witness to the process of creation of the OAU, I can attest to the critical role Haile Selassie played in its success.

## Chapter 11: Turning of the Tide: A Shaken Emperor on the Horns of a Dilemma

1. Kalekristos Abai, a former member of the emperor's bodyguard, wrote his memoirs (in Amharic) on the 1960 attempted coup, in which he gives a list of names that the coup

makers had planned to make up a cabinet of ministers. The author's name figures in the list (at p. 142).

2. Bahru Zewde, "Hayla-Sellase," 107.

## Chapter 12: Last Days: Revolution and the End of the Monarchy

1. Bahru Zewde, "Hayla-Sellase," 109.

## Conclusion

1. Bahru Zewde, "Hayla-Sellase," 101.

# Selected Bibliography


Abbink, Jon. "The Organization and Observation of Elections in Federal Ethiopia: Retrospect and Prospect." In *Election Observation and Democratization in Africa*, edited by Jon Abbink and Gerti Hesseling, 150–79. Basingstoke: Macmillan, 1999. Accessed June 12, 2013. Africa-Wide Information, EBSCOhost.

———. "Religion in Public Spaces: Emerging Muslim-Christian Polemics in Ethiopia." *African Affairs* 110, no. 439 (2011): 253–74.

Abraham, Emmanuel. *Reminiscences of My Life*. Rev. and updated, 1st American ed. Trenton, NJ: Red Sea Press, 2011.

Almagor, Uri. "The Year of the Emperor and the Elephant among the Dassanetch of Ethiopia." *Northeast African Studies* 7, no. 1 (2000): 1–22.

Araia, Ghelawdewos. *Ethiopia: The Political Economy of Transition*. Accessed June 12, 2013. Lanham, MD: University Press of America, 1995. Africa-Wide Information, EBSCOhost.

Asfaw, Kumsa. "Ethiopia, Revolution and the National Question: The Case of the Oromos." *Journal of African Studies* 15, nos. 1–2 (1988): 16–22.

Bahru Zewde. "Hayla-Sellase: From Progressive to Reactionary." *Northeast African Studies* 2, no. 2 (1995): 99–114.

Bedasse, Monique. "Rasta Evolution: The Theology of the Twelve Tribes of Israel." *Journal of Black Studies* 40, no. 5 (2010): 960–73.

Bekele, Getachew. *The Emperor's Clothes: A Personal Viewpoint on Politics and Administration in the Imperial Ethiopian Government, 1941–1974*. East Lansing: Michigan State University Press, 1993.

Bekele, Getnet. "Food Matters: The Place of Development in Building the Postwar Ethiopian State, 1941–1974." *International Journal of African Historical Studies* 42, no. 1 (2009): 29–54.

Bereket Habte Selassie. *The Crown and the Pen: The Memoirs of a Lawyer Turned Rebel*. Trenton, NJ: Red Sea Press, 2007.

Berhanu, Abebe. "The Haile Selassie I Prize Trust." *Northeast African Studies* 2, no. 3 (1995): 53–66.

Beseat, Kiflé Sélassié. "Convaincre, controler ou contraindre? Systèmes et mécanismes de contrôles du pouvoir en Afrique." *Présence africaine: Revue culturelle du monde noir*, nos. 127–128 (1983): 79–113. Accessed June 12, 2013. Africa-Wide Information, EBSCOhost.

Campbell, Ian. *The Plot to Kill Graziani*. Addis Ababa: Addis Ababa University Press, 2010.

Clapham, Christopher. *Haile Selassie's Government*. London: Longmans, 1969.

———. "How Many Ethiopians?" *Africa* 63, no. 1 (1993): 118–28.

Coleman, Sterling Joseph, Jr. "Gradual Abolition or Immediate Abolition of Slavery? The Political, Social, and Economic Quandary of Emperor Haile Selassie I." *Slavery and Abolition* 29, no. 1 (2008): 65–82. Accessed June 12, 2013. Historical Abstracts, EBSCOhost.

Copley, Gregory R. *Ethiopia Reaches Her Hand unto God: Imperial Ethiopia's Unique Symbols, Structures, and*

*Role in the Modern World.* Alexandria, VA.: Defense and Foreign Affairs, International Strategic Studies Association, 1998.

Courtlander, Harold. "The Emperor Wore Clothes: Visiting Haile Selassie in 1943." *American Scholar* 58, no. 2 (1989): 271. Accessed June 12, 2013. Historical Abstracts, EBSCOhost.

De Bono, Emilio. *Anno XIII: The Conquest of an Empire.* London: Cresset Press, 1937.

D'Souza, P. P. "The Ethiopian Parliament: Origin and Evolution." *Africa Quarterly* 20, nos. 3–4 (1981): 19–29. Accessed June 12, 2013. Historical Abstracts, EBSCOhost.

Erlich, Haggai. "Haile Selassie and the Arabs, 1935–1936." *Northeast African Studies* 1, no. 1 (1994): 47–61.

Farago, Ladislas. *Abyssinia on the Eve.* New York: Putnam, 1935.

Gebeyehu, Temesgen. "The Genesis and Evolution of the Ethiopian Revolution and the *Derg*: A Note on Publications by Participants in Events." *History in Africa* 37 (2010): 321–27. Accessed June 12, 2013: Historical Abstracts, EBSCOhost.

Gebissa, Ezekiel. "The Italian Invasion, the Ethiopian Empire, and Oromo Nationalism: The Significance of the Western Oromo Confederation of 1936." *Northeast African Studies* 9, no. 3 (2002): 75–96.

Gebrekidan, Fikru Negash. *Bond without Blood: A History of Ethiopian and New World Black Relations, 1896–1991.* Trenton, NJ: Africa World Press, 2005.

Getachew, Indrias. *Beyond the Throne: The Enduring Legacy of Emperor Haile Selassie I.* Addis Ababa: Shama Books, 2001.

Girma, Amare. "Education and Society in Pre-revolutionary Ethiopia." *Northeast African Studies* 6, nos. 1–2 (1984): 61–79.

Haile Selassie. *My Life and Ethiopia's Progress: The Autobiography of Emperor Haile Selassie I.* 2 vols. Oxford: Oxford University Press, 1976.

Imru Haile Selassie. *Kayehut, Kemastawsew.* Addis Ababa: Addis Ababa University Press, 2010.

Jacobs, Virginia Lee. *Roots of Ras Tafari.* San Diego: Avant Books, 1985.

Juniac, Contran. *Le dernier roi des rois.* Paris: Plon, 1979.

Kapuscinski, Ryszard. *The Emperor.* New ed. London: Penguin, 2006.

Keller, Edmond J. "Ethiopia: Revolution, Class, and National Question." *African Affairs* 80, no. 321 (1981): 519–49.

Larebo, Haile Mariam. "The Ethiopian Orthodox Church and Politics in the Twentieth Century: Part II." *Northeast African Studies* 10, no. 1 (1988): 1–23.

Legum, Colin. *Ethiopia: The Fall of Haile Selassie's Empire.* New York: Africana, 1975.

Levine, Donald. *Greater Ethiopia: A Multiethnic Society.* Chicago: University of Chicago Press, 2000.

Lockot, Hans Wilhelm. *The Mission: The Life, Reign, and Character of Haile Selassie I.* London: Hurst, 1989.

Lyons, Terrence. "The United States and Ethiopia: the Politics of a Patron-Client Relationship." *Northeast African Studies* 8, nos. 2–3 (1986): 53–75.

Makonnen Tegegn. "Walda-Giyorgis Walda-Yohannes and the Haile Sellassie Government." *Northeast African Studies* 4, no. 2 (1997): 91–138.

Mandela, Nelson. *Long Walk to Freedom: The Autobiography of Nelson Mandela.* Boston: Little, Brown, 1994.

Marcus, Harold G. *Haile Selassie I: The Formative Years, 1982–1936.* Berkeley: University of California Press, 1987.

Mcvety, Amanda Kay. "Pursuing Progress: Point Four in Ethiopa." *Diplomatic History* 32, no. 3 (2008): 371–403.

Milkia, Paulos. *Haile Selassie, Western Education, and Political Revolution in Ethiopia.* Youngstown, NY: Cambria Press, 2006.

Mockler, Anthony. *Haile Selassie's War.* New York: Olive Branch Press, 2002.

Monfreid, Henri de. *Le masque d'or, ou Le dernier négus.* Paris: B. Grasset, 1936.

———. *Ménélik tel qu'il fut.* Paris: B. Grasset, 1954.

Mosley, Leonard. *Haile Selassie: The Conquering Lion.* London: Weidenfeld and Nicolson, 1964.

Pankhurst, Richard. "Emperor Haile Sellassie's Arrival in Britain: An Alternative Autobiographical Draft by Percy Arnold." *Northeast African Studies* 9, no. 2 (2002): 1–46.

Prouty, Chris. *Empress Taytu and Menilek II: Ethiopia 1883–1910.* Trenton, NJ: Red Sea Press, 1986.

Rey, C. F. *In the Country of the Blue Nile.* London: Duckworth, 1927.

Sandford, Christine Lush. *Ethiopia under Hailé Selassié.* London: J. M. Dent, 1946.

Schwab, Peter. *Haile Selassie I: Ethiopia's Lion of Judah.* Chicago: Nelson-Hall, 1979.

Shehim, Kassim. "Ethiopia, Revolution, and the Question of Nationalities: The Case of Afar." *Journal of Modern African Studies* 23, no. 2 (1985): 331–48.

Steer, George L. *Caesar in Abyssinia.* London: Hodder and Stoughton, 1936.

Thesiger, Wilfred. *The Life of My Choice.* London: Collins, 1987.

Vestal, Theodore M. *The Lion of Judah in the New World: Emperor Haile Selassie of Ethiopia and the Shaping of Americans' Attitude toward Africa.* Santa Barbara, CA: Praeger, 2011.

# Index

CPSIA information can be obtained
at www.ICGtesting.com
Printed in the USA
FFOW03n1357220817
38964FF